Teaching Your
SECONDARY ELLs
THE ACADEMIC
LANGUAGE *of* TESTS

FOCUSING ON LANGUAGE IN MATHEMATICS, SCIENCE, AND SOCIAL STUDIES

Solution Tree | Press

a division of

Solution Tree

r4 *Educated Solutions*

Educated Solutions

Published by Solution Tree Press

555 North Morton Street
Bloomington, IN 47404
800.733.6786 (toll free) / 812.336.7700
FAX: 812.336.7790

email: info@solution-tree.com
solution-tree.com

Printed in the United States of America

Library of Congress Number:

13 12 11 10 09   1 2 3 4 5

Library of Congress Cataloging-in-Publication Data

Teaching your secondary English language learners the academic language of tests : focusing on language in mathematics, science, and social studies.
    p. cm.
  Includes bibliographical references.
  ISBN 978-1-934009-71-0 (perfect bound) -- ISBN 978-1-935249-04-7 (library bdg.) 1. English language--Study and teaching (Secondary)--Foreign speakers. 2. English language--Study and teaching (Secondary)--Spanish speakers. 3. Vocabulary--Study and teaching (Secondary) 4. Mathematics--Terminology. 5. Science--Terminology. 6. Social sciences--Terminology. 7. Test-taking skills--Study and teaching (Secondary)
  PE1128.A2T448 2009
  428.2'4--dc22
                        2009008189

President: Douglas Rife
Publisher: Robert D. Clouse
Director of Production: Gretchen Knapp
Managing Editor of Production: Caroline Wise
Copy Editor: Nancy Sixsmith
Proofreader: Elisabeth Abrams
Text Designer: Amy Shock
Cover Designer: Pamela Rude

Acknowledgments

r4 Educated Solutions would like to acknowledge the dedication of the many Region 4 content area specialists and external reviewers who devoted time to the development of this book. Their expertise and commitment to children produced this resource to assist educators with quality, effective classroom instruction for English language learners.

Visit **go.solution-tree.com/ELL** to download all the reproducibles in this book.

Table of Contents

Italicized entries in the Table of Contents indicate reproducible forms.

Chapter 2

Chapter 3

Appendices

About r4 Educated Solutions

r4 Educated Solutions is a first-choice provider for the needs of educators, schools, and districts, from cutting-edge instructional materials to assessment data visualization to efficient food service training to inventive transportation solutions. r4 Educated Solutions products and services are developed, field-tested, and implemented by the Region 4 Education Service Center (Region 4).

Region 4, located in Houston, Texas, is one of twenty service centers established by the Texas Legislature in 1967. The service centers assist school districts in improving student performance, enable school districts to operate more efficiently and economically, and implement state initiatives. Encompassing seven counties in the upper Texas Gulf Coast area, Region 4 serves fifty-four independent school districts and forty-nine state-approved charter schools. As the largest service center in Texas, Region 4 serves an educational community of over 1,000,000 students (almost one-fourth of the state's total student population), more than 83,000 professional educators, and approximately 1,300 campuses.

The core purpose of Region 4 is revolutionizing education to inspire and advance future generations. Instructional materials such as this publication are written and reviewed by content-area specialists who have an array of experience in providing quality, effective classroom instruction that provides the most impact on student achievement.

Introduction

If only they understood the question, they could answer it. They know the content, they just don't know enough English.

Teaching Your Secondary English Language Learners the Academic Language of Tests: Focusing on Language in Mathematics, Science, and Social Studies came about in response to remarks similar to the one above. The purpose of this book is twofold: to provide evidence-based, teacher-friendly lesson plans that will help English language learners (ELLs) deal with unfamiliar language features on standardized test questions, and to support content-area teachers in providing instruction for content-specific language skills. This book is geared toward secondary students in grades 6–12 and contains the content areas of math, science, and social studies. Strategies for teaching English language learners the academic language of tests for the English language arts can be found in *Teaching Your Secondary English Language Learners the Academic Language of Tests: Focusing on English Language Arts*, also developed by r4 Educated Solutions.

Each lesson plan provides background information for the teacher, implications for high-stakes testing, a goal, a list of materials, activities, and in many cases, graphic organizers. Some of the lesson plans support learning the language needed to gain content knowledge necessary to prepare for high-stakes tests. Other lessons deal specifically with test language and support instruction on test items. The teaching strategies included in this book are varied and differentiated in order to meet the needs of English language learners. The word lists are divided by content area and grade level, with separate lists for middle and high school students. Included with the word lists are teaching ideas for using the lists in the classroom.

Because the most common unfamiliar item in test questions is vocabulary, the appendix contains a list of academic language vocabulary for each of the three tested content areas. These vocabulary words were compiled from three sources: The *Academic Word List* from the School of Linguistics and Applied Language Studies (Victoria University of Wellington, New Zealand); *Building Academic Vocabulary*, by Robert J. Marzano; and questions from the Texas Assessment of Know-ledge and Skills—Math, Science, and Social Studies. These words are not content vocabulary that is already being taught; instead they make up an academic vocabulary that is necessary to understand the questions being asked. The term *academic English* is based on Jim Cummins' theory of language proficiency, which states that there is a distinction between conversational and academic language (Cummins, 1983).

This manual draws from what the U.S. Department of Education calls professional wisdom, "the judgment that individuals acquire through experience" (Whitehurst, 2002). The foundation of solid professional wisdom can provide valuable insights into effective practice. r4 Educated Solutions presents this book in the hope that it will support and assist teachers as they work to instruct the English language learners in their classrooms.

Chapter 1

The Language of Math

Comparatives

The grammatical structure of a math problem differs greatly from grammar structures used in everyday speech. Of particular importance, and often a primary source of confusion for English language learners, are comparatives (for example, *small, smaller; fast, faster*).

Implications for High-Stakes Testing

Many mathematics test questions require students to compare given information to determine the correct answer. Without understanding the concept of comparatives, as well as the associated vocabulary, students cannot complete the mathematical processing necessary for solving the problem.

Lesson Plan for Comparatives

Materials

- Yarn, in different colors, cut to varying lengths, three or four pieces per group

- Miscellaneous objects (such as school supplies), two per group

Activities

1. To introduce the concept of comparatives, write *Comparatives* and the words *tall, taller,* and *than* on the board. Have four students of different heights stand up. Compare using the following framework: "Joe is tall, but Lee is taller. Mary is taller than Lee. Bill is taller than Mary." Write these sentences on the board, underlining the suffix *-er*. Explain that the *-er* suffix means "more." Just as the heights of the students were compared, comparatives in math problems compare two things with each other.

---

2. Now underline the word *than* in the sentences on the board. Explain that the word *than* is used after a comparative that ends in *-er*, as in "Bill is taller <u>than</u> Mary." Explain the difference between the word *than* and the word *then*. *Than* is used to compare objects. *Then* is used to connect statements or ideas or to indicate a period in time.

3. Now write the words *short, shorter, long, longer,* and *than* in a list on the board. After forming groups of no more than four students, give each group three or four pieces of different-colored yarn, each one cut to a different length. Tell students that they will write sentences comparing the pieces of yarn, using the words on the board. Model a sample sentence, such as, "The green yarn is shorter than the blue yarn." Have groups begin working to write their sentences. **Note:** Depending on the level of the students, a teacher may need to model all the sentences, writing them on the board and having the students copy them.

4. Next, give each of the groups two different objects. These objects might include a book and a pencil, an eraser and a block, or a cup and a pair of scissors. Brainstorm words used to compare objects that the students can use in their writing.

   Examples:

big	bigger
large	larger
light	lighter
little	littler
long	longer
short	shorter
small	smaller

   Ask the groups to compare their objects (for example, which one is bigger, which one is smaller, and so on) and create sentences. Provide the following example for students to use:

   The _____ is _____ than the _____.

5. Ask the students to share their sentences with the whole group. Ask what they notice about the word that compares the two objects. Students should note the *-er* ending. The teacher should also point out the word *than* in the sentences to reinforce its use.

6. Explain how to construct the comparative form in English. Explain that when adjectives are used to compare two things, *-er* is added to the end of the adjective if it has one syllable.

fast	faster
high	higher
low	lower

Also, *-er* is added to the end of the adjective if it has two syllables and ends in *-y* (change the *-y* to an *-i* before adding the *-er* ending).

happy	happier
lonely	lonelier
pretty	prettier

More is used before the adjective if it has two syllables or more.

beautiful	more beautiful
difficult	more difficult
expensive	more expensive

7. Explain that there are a few exceptions to the rule. The two most important exceptions are the adjectives *good* and *bad*.

good	better	best
bad	worse	worst

8. Next, provide examples of questions that use comparatives, such as the following:

   - **Which is faster, the car or the boat?**
   - **Which is better, chocolate or vanilla?**
   - **Which is nearer, Los Angeles or Chicago?**
   - **Which is safer, travel by car or by airplane?**
   - **Which is slower, a tortoise or a hare?**
   - **Which is worse, push-ups or sit-ups?**
   - **Which is higher, the merry-go-round or the Ferris wheel?**

9. Ask the students to go back to their objects and create the questions that could be asked to match the answers they have written, using the previous examples. Have the groups share their questions.

10.   To reinforce the concept, have students play a Twenty Questions guessing game.

Twenty Questions Rules

1.   Choose a student to be the player.

2.   The player chooses an object in the room, but tells only the teacher, not the other students, what the object is.

3.   In order to discover the identity of the object, the students are allowed to ask the player twenty questions that can be answered only with "yes" or "no," including questions that contain comparatives, such as "Is it bigger than a book?" or "Is it smaller than a pencil?" **Note:** Not all questions will contain comparatives.

4.   The player truthfully answers each question in turn.

5.   If a student guesses the object correctly, that student wins and becomes the player for the next round.

6.   If twenty questions are asked without a correct guess, the player wins and gets to be the player for another round.

Superlatives

Superlatives (such as *best*, *longest*, and *smallest*) are frequently used in math problems. They may be a source of confusion for English language learners.

Implications for High-Stakes Testing

Many mathematics test questions require students to identify the "most" or "least" of a particular quality, or to determine the "best" answer to the question. Without understanding the concept of superlatives, as well as the associated vocabulary, students cannot complete the mathematical processing necessary to solve the problem.

Lesson Plan for Superlatives

Materials

- The Superlative Game (page 8), one teacher copy
- The Superlative Game Cards (page 19), one set per group
- Math textbooks, one per student
- Math problems from a state or provincial assessment

Activities

1. Review the lesson of comparatives with the students. Write the word *Comparatives* and the words *tall, taller,* and *tallest* on the board. Have the four students who participated in the height comparatives lesson stand up. Compare the students, using the following framework: "Joe is tall, but Lee is taller. Mary is taller than Lee. Bill is taller than Mary. Bill is the tallest." Write this sentence on the board, underlining the suffix *-est*. Explain that the word *tallest* means "the most tall."

2. Now write the word *Superlatives* on the board. Explain that when something is unique because it is the most or least of a particular quality, the suffix *-est* is added to the end of the adjective describing it, and the word *the* is used before the word because it describes something unique.

3. Now ask, "Who is the shortest?" Write the sentence, "Joe is the shortest" on the board. Again underline the suffix *-est*. Explain that both the words *tall* and *short* are one-syllable words. Superlatives of one-syllable words are formed by adding *-est* to the end of the word.

4. Ask, "Who is the prettiest?" and "Who is the funniest?" and write the corresponding sentences on the board, underlining the suffix *-est*. Explain that two-syllable words that end in *-y* also get the *-est* suffix added at the end, as in *prettiest* and *funniest*.

5. Now write the words *intelligent* and *interesting* on the board. Explain that these words have more than two syllables, so instead of adding the suffix *-est* to the end of the word, the word *most* is used in front of the word. Ask, "Who is the most intelligent?" and "Who is the most interesting?" Write these sentences on the board, underlining the words *the* and *most*.

6. To the list of comparatives from the previous lesson, add the superlative forms of the following words:

big	bigger	biggest
beautiful	more beautiful	most beautiful
expensive	more expensive	most expensive
fat	fatter	fattest
happy	happier	happiest
high	higher	highest
intelligent	more intelligent	most intelligent
lonely	lonelier	loneliest
low	lower	lowest
near	nearer	nearest
pretty	prettier	prettiest

7. Form groups of five to seven students to play the Superlative Game, a fun game that will get the students laughing and interacting. Give each group a set of eight Superlative Game Cards. Have each student in the group choose one word to represent. Do not tell them that each word represents a specific funny task. The students will assume they are representing the word literally. The words on the cards are the following:

widest	highest
longest	funniest
shortest	biggest
most	fastest

8. Other words can be added or substituted by the teacher, depending on the students.

9. After each student has chosen a superlative to represent, have the representatives for the first word come to the front of the room. Ask the students to do the funny task listed on the Superlative Game Task List. For example, when the representatives for the word *widest* come to the front of the room, ask them who can spread their arms the widest. Measure their arm spans with a yardstick and declare a winner. Say, "Monica is the widest. Now, who is the longest?" Continue the game with the rest of the words until all the funny tasks have been completed and a winner is named in every superlative category.

10. Explain to students that *good* and *bad* are exceptions to the rules for superlatives, just as they were for comparatives.

good	better	best
bad	worse	worst

11. After students are successful in the small groups, have them work individually, going through their math textbook and finding examples of word problems that contain superlatives. As an extension of the lesson, have students find superlatives in math problems from a state or provincial assessment.

The Superlative Game

1. Form groups of five to seven students to play the Superlative Game.

2. Give each group a set of The Superlative Game Cards (page 19) and have each student in the group choose a word to represent. (Other words can be added or substituted by the teacher, depending on the students' needs.) Do not reveal that each word represents a funny challenge.

3. After each student has chosen a superlative, have the representatives for the first word come to the front of the room together. Ask the students to do the funny task listed on the Superlative Game Task List (see table 1.1). For example, when the representatives for the word *widest* come to the front of the room, ask them who can spread their arms the widest. Measure their arm spans with a yardstick and declare a winner. Say, "Monica is the widest. Now, who is the longest?"

4. Continue the game with the rest of the words until all the tasks have been completed and a winner is named in every superlative category.

Table 1.1: The Superlative Game Task List

Category	Task
widest	spread arms
longest	hold breath
shortest	measure pencil
most	count buttons
highest	raise eyebrows
funniest	make facial expression
biggest	smile
fastest	say: "She sells seashells by the seashore."

Prepositions

Many languages do not use prepositions as a part of speech. In English mathematics, word problems frequently contain prepositions or prepositional phrases that provide clues to the operations required to solve problems. Without knowledge of these prepositions, students lack the language skills necessary for successful problem solving.

Implications for High-Stakes Testing

Students must understand the function of prepositions in math word problems in order to successfully determine which operations to use to solve the problem.

Lesson Plan for Prepositions

Materials

- Preposition List handout (page 20), one per student

- Operation and Problem Note Cards from pages 21–22 (printed on two different-colored note cards, as detailed in Step 5), one set per group

- Phrase and Mathematical Symbol Note Cards from pages 23–24 (printed on two different-colored note cards, as detailed in Step 9), one set per group

- *Inside, Outside, Upside Down*, by Stan and Jan Berenstain

- Envelopes, one per group for the Operation Note Cards and one per group for the Problem Note Cards

- Math questions from a state or provincial assessment or other series of word problems

Activities

1. Pass out a copy of the Preposition List to each student, and review prepositions with them. Explain that prepositions are used in English with a noun to show time, place, or other relationships, and many prepositions have more than one meaning.

2. Read the book *Inside, Outside, Upside Down*, by Stan and Jan Berenstain, as a way to introduce prepositions. Identify each preposition while reading, and discuss its purpose.

3. Explain to students that in math, prepositions are used for the same reasons they are used in the book, and they are also used at times to help determine which operation should be used to solve problems.

4. To introduce this concept, focus on the preposition *by*. Tell students that the preposition *by* could mean many different things in word problems. The preposition *by* alone does not tell which operation to use, but when used in conjunction with other words, different operations may be apparent. Explain that the preposition *by* could mean the following:

   - *Next to* (no operation required)

   - *According to* (no operation required)

   - *How* (no operation required)

   - *Which number to divide* (10 *by* 2)

   - *Which number to multiply* (4 *by* 7)

- *Area* (50 feet *by* 20 feet)

- *Volume* (5 feet high *by* 2 feet wide *by* 5 feet long)

- *Which number to add* (increased *by*, exceeds *by*)

- *Which number to subtract* (decreased *by*)

5. After forming groups of two to four students, give each group an envelope containing note cards as described as follows. The note cards should be two different colors—one for the operation and one for the problem—and they should be shuffled. One note card is intentionally left blank for the students to fill in. Tell students to match the word problem with the operation that *by* suggests. Ask them, "What does the word *by* mean in the following examples?"

Color A: Operation

- Next to—no operation

- How—no operation

- According to—no operation

- Which number to divide

- Which number to multiply

- Which number to add

- Which number to subtract

Color B: Problem

- When standing in order from oldest to youngest, June is *by* Bob, and Bob is *by* Sally. If June is 16, which of the following statements cannot be true?

- Mrs. Gold designed a piece of art *by* outlining equilateral triangles with wire. How much wire did Mrs. Gold use to complete her piece of art?

- Which statement is supported *by* the graph?

- Mrs. Jones wants to divide her eggs into equal groups *by* placing them into six containers. If she has 36 eggs, how many eggs will go into each container?

- When x is multiplied *by* 2, the answer is 10 more than 20. What is x?

- Mr. Smith wants to plant grass in his yard. The rectangular backyard is 100 feet *by* 80 feet. What is the area of the backyard that will be planted with grass?

- If x exceeds 2 *by* 7, what is x?

- Bill spends $125 each month on clothes. If he decreases his spending *by* $15 each month, how much money will he save in a year?

6. After students have had the opportunity to match the operations to the problems, review their answers, and discuss how the preposition *by* provided signals and what it signaled.

7. Using a state or provincial assessment (or other series of word problems), give each group an envelope with sample problems that contain the same preposition. For example, one group would have problems using *into*, one group would have problems with *for*, one group would have problems with *at*, and so on. (A test from a lower grade level might be a better resource so students can focus on the language instead of the math concepts.) Have students analyze their problems, seeking to determine which operation, if any, their preposition signals in each of the problems. The groups should be prepared to share this with the class.

8. For English language learners, one of the most difficult prepositions to understand, and one most frequently used, is the preposition *of*. In math, as in English, *of* is a signal that introduces an object. Write the expressions and equations that follow on the board. Also note the use of the conjunction *and* in these expressions.

   - The product *of* five and seven: $(5)(7)$

   - The sum *of* five and seven: $5 + 7$

   - The product *of* two and a number: $2(x)$

   - The area *of* a rectangle: the product *of* length and width

   Examine how *of* specifies one or more objects or numbers.

9. Give the students note cards (two colors—mathematical symbols on one color and phrases on another) and have them match the *of* prepositional phrase with the mathematical symbol it signals.

Color C: Phrases

- The opposite *of* 1
- The absolute value *of* 2
- The reciprocal *of* 3
- Half *of* 4

- The square *of* 5
- The cube *of* 6
- The square root *of* 9

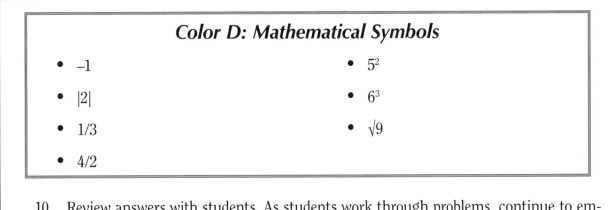

10. Review answers with students. As students work through problems, continue to emphasize the signals that prepositions provide.

Passive Voice

Math word problems often   sentences that use the passive voice. English language learners often have difficulty with this structure because of vocabulary constraints, and often cannot successfully determine the action and the actor.

Implications for High-Stakes Testing

Understanding the story of math word problems is essential in order to successfully solve the problem. Students must be able to determine the actor and action in order to perform the correct computations.

Lesson Plan for Passive Voice

Materials

- Puzzle Piece Sentences (pages 25–26), one set per pair

  Before the class period, the teacher must create puzzle pieces for the activity. Cut the cards in half using varying patterns to create puzzle pieces. It is important that no two cards have the same cut, or the activity will not be successful. On the left side of the card, write a passive sentence. On the right side of the card, write the corresponding active sentence. Examples are given at the end of the lesson plan.

- Passive to Active Sentences (page 27), one copy per pair

Activities

1. Group students into pairs, and give each pair a set of the puzzle pieces. Say to students: **I am giving you several sets of sentences. The two sentences in each set will give the same information, but will be written in a different way. Your task is to match the sentences that go together. If you are correct, your pieces will fit together.** Allow students time to work together to match their sentences.

2. After students have matched their sentences, ask them to make observations about the two different types of sentences on the puzzle pieces. Allow five minutes for students to draw their conclusions. Once time has expired, have each pair share observations. Students should note the location of the nouns, "to be" verbs, and so on.

3. Explain that the passive voice is used when focusing on the person or thing affected by an action. The passive voice is most often used when the object of the action is more important than who or what is performing the action. The passive is formed by using the following:

Passive Subject	+ "To Be" Verb	+ Past Participle	+ By	+ Performer of the Action
The house	was	bought	by	the teacher.
The fence	was	painted	by	the boy.

4. Give students the Passive to Active Sentences handout, and have them rewrite them in the active voice. Depending on the proficiency of students, they can complete this activity on their own or in pairs. Once completed, review the sentences in the whole group.

5. Explain that many math word problems contain passive voice statements. Stress that it is important to pay attention to the action and the actor in order to successfully understand what the problem is asking.

Reversals

In English mathematics, word problems frequently contain reversals such as "The number a is 5 less than b." Though the correct equation is $a = b - 5$, English language learners frequently interpret the wording as $a = 5 - b$. Students must understand the structure of the sentence in order to understand the computations required.

Implications for High-Stakes Testing

In order to successfully solve problems on standardized math tests, students must be able to negotiate the meanings of words and phrases that indicate specific calculations.

Lesson Plan for Reversals

Materials

TV Guide Chart (page 28), copied on a transparency or computer slide

Activities

1. Using the overhead, show students the blank TV Guide Chart, and ask them to help fill in the times based on the information listed above the chart.

2. Review the correct schedule of television programs.

7:00	8:00	9:00	10:00
Ugly Betty	Gossip Girl	Heroes	The Hills

3. Ask students why *Ugly Betty* is listed before *Gossip Girl* on the schedule even though *Gossip Girl* is listed first. Students should be able to point out that the phrase ". . . is on later than" signals that the shows are reversed. Explain to the students that this is called a *reversal*. You might draw an arrow from the program named first in the sentence that ends after the second program to make this point visually.

Gossip Girl is on later than *Ugly Betty.*

4. Continue this method with all examples listed on the board.

5. Explain to students that math word problems sometimes contain reversals, too. The reversal phrase found in math problems that is most similar to *later than* used in the TV Guide example is *less than*. This phrase signals that numbers in a number sentence will be in a different order than they are in the word problem. Give the following example:

    The number 90 is 10 less than 100.

6. Write the number sentence for the preceding problem, using arrows to show how the numbers are reversed. Stress the phrase *less than* and point out how it changes the order of the number sentence in comparison with the word problem.

    The number 90 is 10 less than 100.

    $$90 = 100-10$$

7. Give students several examples of similar problems, asking them to show the number sentence for each problem.

Conditionals

Conditionals are a common text structure in math word problems and are written in the form of *if . . . then* statements. *Condition* means "situation or circumstance." If a particular condition is true, then a particular result happens. Conditionals are sometimes called *if* structures or sentences because the word *if* usually (but not always) occurs in a conditional sentence.

Implications for High-Stakes Testing

Many math word problems contain conditional statements that must be understood in order to successfully solve the problem. Students unfamiliar with this structure cannot determine the meaning of the word problem. Students must understand the conditional (or *if*) structure in order to solve the problems.

Lesson Plan for Conditionals

Materials

- Million-Dollar Checks (page 29), one per student with the student's name on it

- Red and green dry-erase or overhead markers for teacher use

- Red and green markers or map pencils, one set per student

- Math problems containing conditionals from a state or provincial assessment, or other math problems using conditionals, one per student

Activities

1. Pass out a Million-Dollar Check to each student and ask them to think about what they would do if the check were real. How would they spend a million dollars?

2. Put the following statements on the board or overhead, and ask students to complete them individually:

   - *If I had a million dollars, then I would _____ .*

   - *If I had a million dollars and had to give it to my school, then it would go to _____ (name of school).*

3. Ask individual students to share their answers to the "If I had a million dollars" question with the whole group. Record these responses on the board or overhead. Note how the students' answers differ. Then ask students for their answers to the second question. Note that they all now have the same answer.

---

4. Explain to students that *if . . . then* statements are very important because they show the conditions under which certain things occur, or happen. **Condition means "situation or circumstance." If a particular condition is true,** *then* **a particular result happens.** Explain that conditional sentences are sometimes called *if* sentences because the word *if* usually occurs in a conditional sentence.

5. Use the analogy that *if . . . then* statements are like a stop light. **The** *if* **part of the sentence, or conditional clause, is the red light, or the condition given.** Draw a red line under the *if* part of the sentences on the board or overhead. **The** *then* **part of the sentence, the main clause, is the green light, or the action.** Draw a green line under the *then* part of the sentences on the board or overhead. Draw arrows from the *if* to the *then* on the sentences on the board or overhead. Also, show how the statements can be reversed: "*If* I had a million dollars and had to give it to my school, *then* it would go to . . . " changes to "The money would go to ABC School *if* I had a million dollars and had to give it to my school."

6. Explain that this is true in math word problems. The *if* statement tells the conditions under which the problem can be solved, and the *then* statement shows the action required. Give the following example:

(Point out to the students that the *then* is not always written but sometimes assumed. The *if* gives the conditions [21 buses, 47 band members on each bus] and the *then* shows the action required [how many total on all buses].)

> *Several middle school bands boarded buses after a marching competition. If there were 21 buses and 47 band members on each bus,* then *about how many band members were on the buses in all?*

Underline the *if* statement in red, and the *then* statement in green. Take out the word *then* to demonstrate that the sentence would have the same meaning without the word.

> If *there were 21 buses and about 47 band members on each bus* →*how many band members were on the buses in all?*

Explain that in some cases the *if . . . then* statement is reversed. Give this example:

> *Mrs. Miller is baking cookies for 16 children. She has baked 2 dozen cookies. How many more cookies should Mrs. Miller bake* if *she wants each child to receive exactly 2 cookies and have none left over?*

Point out that in this case, the *if . . . then* statement is reversed. Have students point out the conditional (if) and underline the *if* statement in red. Next have students point out the action required. Underline this in green. Again use arrows to show the relationships.

> *How many more cookies should Mrs. Miller bake* ← *if she wants each child to receive exactly 2 cookies and have none left over?*

7. Using a state or provincial assessment or additional math problems with conditionals, have students underline the *if* statements in red and the *then* statements in green. Ask students to draw arrows from the condition to the action required.

8. For an extension of this lesson, students could write their own word problems using *if . . . then* statements for others to answer.

The Superlative Game Cards

widest	longest
shortest	most
highest	funniest
biggest	fastest

Preposition List

Place

above

across

against

among

around

at

behind

below

beneath

beside

beyond

by

in

inside

into

near

next to

off

on

out

outside

over

through

throughout

toward

under

up

upon

with

without

Time

after

around

at

before

between

by

during

for

from

in

on

since

to

until

within

Relationship

besides

except

like

of

Operation Note Cards

next to (no operation)	how (no operation)
according to (no operation)	which number to divide
which number to multiply	which number to add
which number to subtract	

Teaching Your Secondary ELLs the Academic Language of Tests: Focusing on Language in Mathematics, Science, and Social Studies
© 2009 r4 Educated Solutions • solution-tree.com • Visit go.solution-tree.com/ELL to download this page.

Problem Note Cards

When standing in order from oldest to youngest, June is *by* Bob, and Bob is *by* Sally. If June is 16, which of the following statements cannot be true?	Mrs. Gold designed a piece of art *by* outlining equilateral triangles with wire. How much wire did Mrs. Gold use to complete her piece of art?
Which statement is supported *by* the graph?	Mrs. Jones wants to divide her eggs into equal groups *by* placing them into six containers. If she has 36 eggs, how many eggs will go into each container?
When *x* is multiplied *by* 2, the answer is 10 more than 20. What is *x*?	Mr. Smith wants to plant grass in his yard. The rectangular backyard is 100 feet *by* 80 feet. What is the area of the backyard that will be planted with grass?
If *x* exceeds 2 *by* 7, what is *x*?	Bill spends $125 each month on clothes. If he decreases his spending *by* $15 each month, how much money will he save in a year?

Phrase Note Cards

the opposite of 1	the absolute value of 2
the reciprocal of 3	half of 4
the square of 5	the cube of 6
the square root of 9	

Mathematical Symbol Note Cards

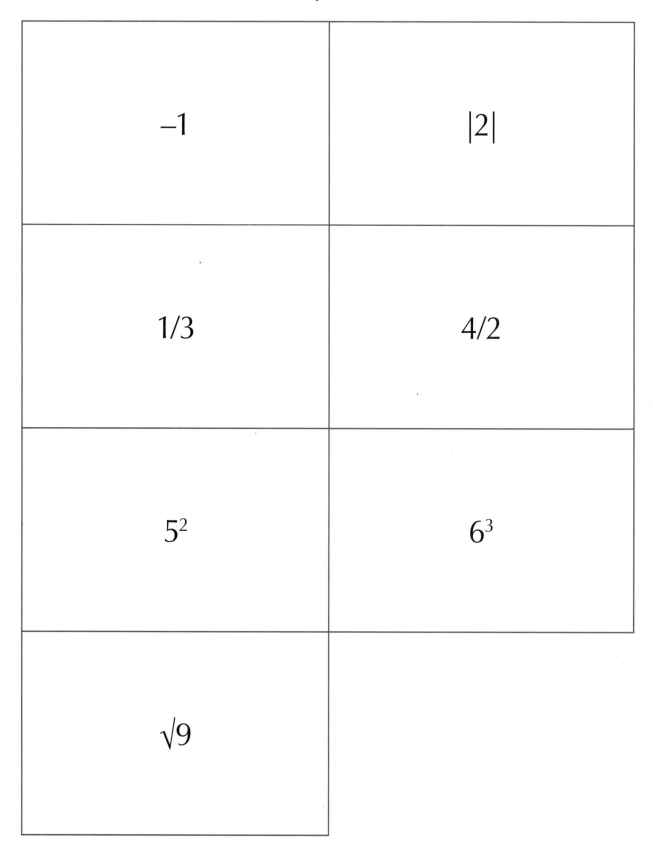

-1	$\lvert 2 \rvert$
$1/3$	$4/2$
5^2	6^3
$\sqrt{9}$	

Puzzle Piece Sentences

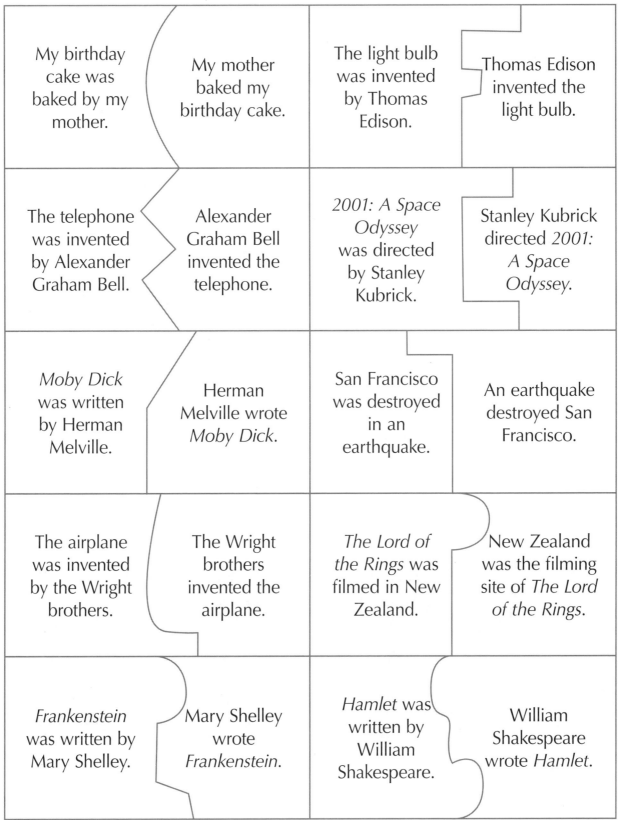

My birthday cake was baked by my mother.

My mother baked my birthday cake.

The light bulb was invented by Thomas Edison.

Thomas Edison invented the light bulb.

The telephone was invented by Alexander Graham Bell.

Alexander Graham Bell invented the telephone.

2001: A Space Odyssey was directed by Stanley Kubrick.

Stanley Kubrick directed *2001: A Space Odyssey*.

Moby Dick was written by Herman Melville.

Herman Melville wrote *Moby Dick*.

San Francisco was destroyed in an earthquake.

An earthquake destroyed San Francisco.

The airplane was invented by the Wright brothers.

The Wright brothers invented the airplane.

The Lord of the Rings was filmed in New Zealand.

New Zealand was the filming site of *The Lord of the Rings*.

Frankenstein was written by Mary Shelley.

Mary Shelley wrote *Frankenstein*.

Hamlet was written by William Shakespeare.

William Shakespeare wrote *Hamlet*.

continued

Puzzle Piece Sentences (continued)

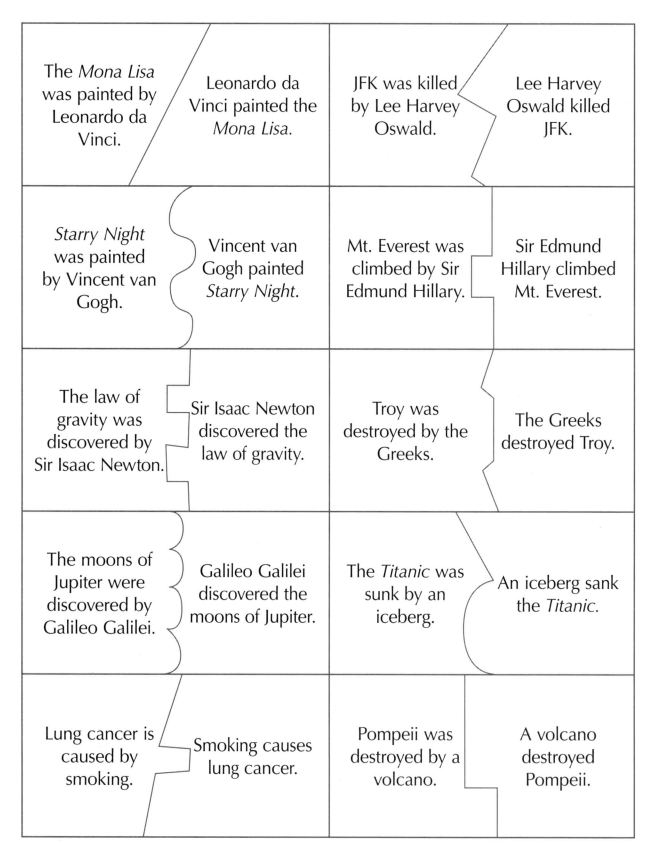

The *Mona Lisa* was painted by Leonardo da Vinci.

Leonardo da Vinci painted the *Mona Lisa*.

JFK was killed by Lee Harvey Oswald.

Lee Harvey Oswald killed JFK.

Starry Night was painted by Vincent van Gogh.

Vincent van Gogh painted *Starry Night*.

Mt. Everest was climbed by Sir Edmund Hillary.

Sir Edmund Hillary climbed Mt. Everest.

The law of gravity was discovered by Sir Isaac Newton.

Sir Isaac Newton discovered the law of gravity.

Troy was destroyed by the Greeks.

The Greeks destroyed Troy.

The moons of Jupiter were discovered by Galileo Galilei.

Galileo Galilei discovered the moons of Jupiter.

The *Titanic* was sunk by an iceberg.

An iceberg sank the *Titanic*.

Lung cancer is caused by smoking.

Smoking causes lung cancer.

Pompeii was destroyed by a volcano.

A volcano destroyed Pompeii.

Passive to Active Sentences

Passive	Active
Cars are made in Detroit.	They make cars in Detroit.
Dinner is being cooked by Dad.	Dad is cooking dinner.
The paints will be used by the class.	The class will use the paints.
The Old Man and the Sea was written by Ernest Hemingway.	Ernest Hemingway wrote *The Old Man and the Sea*.
The answers were shown to the students by the teacher.	
Cell phones were used by all the workers.	
The window was measured by the painter.	
He was placed in a new class by the principal.	
It was chosen by everyone.	
That show is watched by millions.	
The ball was moved by the player.	
The groceries were bought by her mother.	
The movie was shown by the theater.	
The area was settled by immigrants.	
The money was paid by the company.	
The chart was read by the doctor.	

TV Guide Chart

- *Gossip Girl* is on later than *Ugly Betty.*

- *Heroes* is on later than *Gossip Girl.*

- *The Hills* is on later than *Heroes.*

7:00	8:00	9:00	10:00

Million-Dollar Checks

The Money Tree
5800 Growing Street
Green Town, America

Date _____

Pay to the
Order of _____   **$1,000,000**

One Million Dollars and no/100s _____

World's Biggest Bank   100 Gold Avenue
Here, America

whatever you want! _____   *Mr. Money Tree* _____
for

The Money Tree
5800 Growing Street
Green Town, America

Date _____

Pay to the
Order of _____   **$1,000,000**

One Million Dollars and no/100s _____

World's Biggest Bank   100 Gold Avenue
Here, America

whatever you want! _____   *Mr. Money Tree* _____
for

The Money Tree
5800 Growing Street
Green Town, America

Date _____

Pay to the
Order of _____   **$1,000,000**

One Million Dollars and no/100s _____

World's Biggest Bank   100 Gold Avenue
Here, America

whatever you want! _____   *Mr. Money Tree* _____
for

Chapter 2

The Language of Science

Greek and Latin Roots and Affixes

Note: This lesson plan can also be adapted for use in social studies and mathematics classrooms.

Greek and Latin roots and affixes are used extensively in science vocabulary. Students need to have knowledge of these word parts to support the comprehension of written science text and concepts.

Implications for High-Stakes Testing

Limited conceptual knowledge and difficulty in understanding the meanings of words can hinder English language learners' success on high-stakes exams. Understanding Greek and Latin affixes will help students build vocabulary for comprehending more complex text and ideas.

Lesson Plan for Greek and Latin Roots and Affixes

Materials

- Greek and Latin Word Parts List (page 44), one copy per student

- Question Cards (pages 45–47), one set per group

- Word Web handout (page 48), five copies per group

- Word Parts Scavenger Hunt handout (page 49), one copy per student

- Highlighters in two different colors, one set per student

- Dictionaries, one per group

- Science textbook, one per student

Activities

1. Write a word such as *transportation* on the board. Ask students what other words they know that sound similar to this word or that have the same word parts. For example, students might identify *translation, transcontinental, transfer, transpiration,* and so on. (If students are beginning speakers of English, you may have to provide the other words.) Ask what these words have in common (for example, they all contain *trans-*). Ask students if they know what any of these words mean. After a few answers have been given, ask again what they have in common. Explain that *trans-* is a prefix that means *across* or *between*. Using this information, ask them what the other words might mean.

2. Explain that a *prefix* is a small word part that goes at the beginning of a word, a *suffix* is a small word part that goes at the end of a word, and a *root* is a base word whose meaning is changed by adding a prefix and/or a suffix. Give the students a copy of the Greek and Latin Word Parts List, and discuss it with them.

3. Form groups of no more than four students. Give each group several of the Question Cards to help them think about how word parts can help determine meaning. More than one group can have the same card. Tell students to highlight the affixes in one color and the root or base word in a different color. Tell students to be prepared to explain their answers to the class.

4. After all groups have shared, give each group five copies of the Word Web handout and one dictionary. Assign five specific affixes from the chart to each group. Ask students to find words containing their assigned word parts as well as the definitions for these words. Have them construct Word Webs (see figure 2.1).

5. Next, have students complete a scavenger hunt in their science textbook for words. Give students the Word Parts Scavenger Hunt. Write a limited number of word parts on the board. Ask students to find a word that contains one of the Greek or Latin word parts listed and note the context in which it is used. You may also ask students to predict a definition and then look up the word in the textbook glossary to confirm their definition.

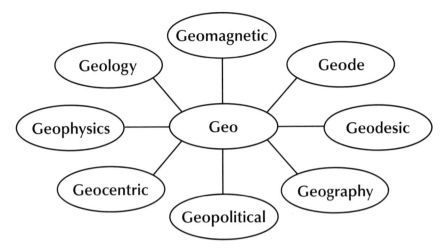

Figure 2.1: This is a sample Word Web for the affix *geo*.

Investigation

Science has a language all its own. In addition to technical vocabulary, this lesson also includes words an English language learner needs to know in order to understand directions, equipment, and processes. Unlike simple vocabulary, most of these words need to be taught in context to be understood.

Implications for High-Stakes Testing

Students must understand various types of vocabulary in order to understand the experiment and/or process questioned in the test.

Lesson Plan for Investigation

Materials

- Chart paper, three sheets per group

- Highlighters or colored pencils in three different colors, one set per group

- Markers, three different colors, one set per group

- Materials for lab, one set per group:

    - Container

    - Carbonated beverage

    - Raisins

    - Lab Report (pages 50–51), one copy per student

Activities

This activity is meant to be an ongoing process. The students should go through the initial procedure as outlined. This process should be used every time students conduct or complete a Lab Report for an investigation.

1. Place students in groups of four. Place the Raising Raisins Investigation transparency on the overhead, and provide students with a copy. Read through the investigation with the whole class.

2. Give each group three sheets of chart paper and three different colored highlighters or colored pencils. Point out to students that some of the words on the handout are underlined, some are italicized, and some are in boldface. Have students highlight these words on their handout, using a different color for each type. After students have finished highlighting, have them record the highlighted words on chart paper, listing words highlighted with the same color together on the same piece of chart paper.

3. After students have grouped the words, ask them to come up with a category title that describes the categorization system they used. Lead students through a discussion that will help them understand that the science vocabulary was coded into three groups: science vocabulary, action vocabulary, and materials vocabulary.

4. Now conduct the investigation. As students go through the investigation, focus on the vocabulary words.

5. For future investigations, continue to use this color-coding process to highlight key vocabulary. As students become more proficient, have them color-code their own investigations.

Raising Raisins Investigation

Bold words are science vocabulary. <u>Underlined</u> words are action vocabulary. *Italic* words are materials.

Problem

What **properties** or changes will *raisins* exhibit when they are <u>exposed</u> to a **gas** in a **liquid**?

Hypothesis

If *raisins* are <u>exposed</u> to a **gas** in a **liquid**, then they <u>absorb</u> the **gas** and explode.

Plan for Raising Raisins Investigation

Materials

- Container
- Carbonated beverage
- Raisins

Procedure

1. <u>Fill</u> the *container* half full of the *carbonated beverage.*

2. <u>Put</u> five *raisins* of different sizes into the *container.*

3. <u>Observe</u> the *raisins*, the **gas**, and the **liquid** for a few minutes. <u>Record</u> the **interactions** between the *raisins*, **gas**, and **liquid.**

Observations

- At the beginning of the experiment, the **liquid** is clear, the **gas** is clear, and the **solids** (*raisins*) are dark brown.

- The **gas** bubbles are <u>adhering</u> to the *raisins*, causing the *raisins* to float up to the top of the **liquid**.

- As the *raisins* reach the top of the **liquid**, some of the bubbles pop, causing the *raisin* to sink back to the bottom of the *container.*

- Smaller *raisins* rise more frequently.

- Larger *raisins* rise less frequently.

Conclusion

<u>Exposing</u> *raisins* to a **gas** in a **liquid** creates apparent changes in the properties of the *raisins.* The lab showed a direct relationship between the *raisins*, the **gas**, and the **liquid.** Although the *raisins* did not <u>absorb</u> the **gas** and explode, the **gas** did make an apparent change in the **physical properties** of the *raisin.*

When the *raisins* were added to the *carbonated drink*, the **carbon dioxide** bubbles immediately began <u>adhering</u> to the **surface** of the *raisins*. As more bubbles clung to the **surface**, the *raisins* began to float to the top of the **liquid**. The bubbles were apparently changing the **density** of the *raisins*, making them less **dense** than the surrounding **liquid** and therefore making them float. As the *raisins* reached the top of the **liquid**, some of the **gas** bubbles popped, and the *raisins* began sinking. With fewer bubbles attached, the *raisins* again were **denser** than the **liquid** and therefore sank back to the bottom of the *container*.

One problem that could be encountered with this lab is that the longer the *raisins* are <u>exposed</u> to the **liquid**, the heavier they become. The **liquid** is being <u>absorbed</u> by the *raisins*, making them plump up. This is apparent as the color of the *raisins* gets lighter after some time.

One question that arose during the investigation was, "Will *raisins* exhibit similar behaviors in different types of *carbonated beverages*?"

Observations

Observations in science must be precise, objective, and accurate. Practicing this skill provides an opportunity for students to develop vocabulary while learning content.

Implications for High-Stakes Testing

Students must be able to make accurate observations using their senses in order to perform proficiently. Students need practice in using observation skills, as well as in using appropriate vocabulary, to be successful.

Lesson Plan for Observations

Materials

- Blank Lab Report, one per student (pages 50–51)

- Transparency of Sample Science Question With Graphic (page 52)

- Three or four postmarked envelopes with handwritten addresses for Station A

- Two boxes (one for Station B and one for Station C)

- Object that makes a sound for Station B, placed inside a sealed box

- Object with texture for Station C, placed inside a slotted box

- Three or four beakers (or other containers) for Station D

- Three or four substances with distinct smells for Station D

- Lab notebook for each student

- Sample Lab Report from a previous lab performed in class, one copy per student (The teacher may need to fill this out to ensure that it contains adequate observations in the results section.)

Note: Although observations generally can involve any or all of the five senses, in secondary science observations, typically only sight, sound, touch, and smell are used. Taste is not used for safety reasons.

Activities

1. Prior to beginning the activity, create four stations for students.

Station A: Envelopes

These should be postmarked and handwritten with addresses in multiple handwriting/styles. They can be torn, bent, and so on. The students will be making visual observations and later inferences to determine the "story" of the envelope.

Station B: What's That Sound?

This is a sealed box with an object inside that makes a sound. Students will make sound observations using this box.

Station C: Inside the Box

This is a box with an object inside that has texture. The box should have a slot for students to place their hand into without seeing inside. The students will feel an object and make tactile observations.

Station D: What's That Smell?

This station consists of three or four containers of substances with different smells. Examples might include perfume, sulfur, vinegar, ammonia, and so on. A range of smells should be provided so that students can make the most observations regarding smell. **Note:** For safety purposes, students should *always* waft, rather than sniff!

2. Divide the students into small groups. Give each student a copy of a sample Lab Report. Each student should also have his or her own lab notebook.

3. Write the word *observation* on the board, and ask students to discuss the question What are observations? in their groups. Have students share ideas with the whole group about observations. Discuss the four senses used in science observations (sight, sound, touch, and smell). Explain that observations are collected not only using sight but also with the other three senses of sound, touch, and smell. Explain that taste is not used for safety reasons. Have students give examples of how and when they have made observations with the other senses of sound, touch, and smell.

4. Explain to students that they will be using their powers of observation to describe the objects in each of the four stations. They must use words and/or phrases that are factual, specific, and objective. Discuss the difference between subjective statements and objective statements. For example, "it smells gross" or "nasty" would be subjective, and therefore not appropriate. "It smells like rotten eggs" might be more appropriate because it is factual and objective.

5. Have students rotate through the stations in their groups, discuss their observations, and then write the group's words or phrases in their lab notebooks. As they rotate through, ask them to use their powers of observation to start forming a hypothesis about each object at the stations. (For example, what type of letter was in the envelope, and what are the objects in the boxes and containers?)

6. After the groups have finished rotating through all four stations, ask students to return to their seats and share with the whole group the lists of observations each group has created. Write their collective observations on the board. Ask students questions about their observations. **Which words/phrases were on more than one list? Which observations were subjective? Which observations were objective? Why do we use objective observations in science?**

7. Now have the students look at the sample Lab Report from a lab previously performed in their class, noting specifically the Results (Data) section. Ask students to locate the words and phrases used by scientists to describe their observations and then to classify them into sight, sound, touch, or smell. Compare the words and phrases from their own observations to the words and phrases used in the sample Lab Report.

8. After students have a firm grasp of the types of scientific observations and the language used to make these observations, show students the Sample Science Question With Graphic on the overhead. Explain that now that they have used their observation skills with objects, they will practice using their visual observation skills with the type of graphic they would see on a standardized science test. Ask students to make observations about the graphic before looking at the question. Then have the students note the types of observations required, as well as the language used in the question, and compare it with their initial observations about the graphic. Ask students to make inferences and discuss the difference between inference and observation. As an extension, students can look at science questions with graphics from a state or provincial assessment or other sources and make the same observations.

Process Explanation

In order to be successful in science class, a student must be able to negotiate meaning and produce language in various activities, including explaining processes. Without specific skills in this area, English language learners may miss fundamental conceptual understanding.

Implications for High-Stakes Testing

When English language learners are able to recognize and understand key terms used to explain processes, they will understand and complete high-stakes test questions successfully.

Lesson Plan for Observations

Materials

- Sample Signal Words handout (page 53), one per student
- Paper Footprints (page 54)
- Sentence strips
- Note cards
- Markers
- Tape

Activities

1. Before class begins, cut out the paper Footprints. (They may be laminated for durability.) Place them in a line starting at the door, going through the room, and going back out the door. At various points along the trail, the Footprints represent havoc (for example, draw on the board, pull books out of the bookshelf, tip over a trashcan, and so on). The premise is that an intruder has been in the class, and students will be the Crime Scene Investigators sent to investigate.

2. After students enter the class, have them determine what has happened in the room. Most will have watched television programs such as *CSI*, so ask them to "reconstruct" the crime. Guide them by asking questions such as what happened first, what happened next, and so on. Write each of their statements on sentence strips, and tape them to the wall. Remind students that their statements must be factual and accurate. Post the statements in the order they are made, but have the students make corrections if they notice events are out of order.

3. After all events are decided upon by the students and recorded on the sentence strips, have the class make sure they are in order. Explain the importance of having clear sentences that are in order. Ask what would happen if they weren't in order or they weren't clear.

4. Tell students that it is now time to clean up the crime scene, but future investigators will need to understand what happened. If the sentence strips are taken down, how will they know what happened first, second, and so on? Ask what words can be used to "signal" when events happened. Have students generate a list, putting each word (or phrase) on a note card. Tape these note cards to the sentence strips to show how they signal the order in which the events occurred. Explain that signal words also help us explain the steps in scientific processes. Ask students to come up with examples from previous class lessons or experiments.

5. After the activity is complete, use the note cards to form a word wall (p. 87) . Give students a copy of the Sample Signal Words handout. Have students write a paragraph describing the crime scene and the events that happened using the signal words from the note cards or those found on the Sample Signal Words handout.

Spanish and English Cognates

Note: This lesson plan can also be adapted for use in social studies and mathematics classrooms.

Cognates are words that are spelled (although not pronounced) identically or nearly identically in Spanish and English.

Table 2.1: Examples of Identical Cognates

Spanish	English
color	color
doctor	doctor
horrible	horrible
hospital	hospital
popular	popular

Table 2.2: Examples of Nearly Identical Cognates

Spanish	English
conversación	conversation
inteligente	intelligent
música	music
programa	program
violencia	violence

Cognates offer Spanish-speaking English language learners a vast wealth of words to add to their English vocabularies. While the concept may seem obvious to the teacher, it is not usually noticed by ELLs independently. In fact, many ELLs have a difficult time grasping even exact cognates due to the pronunciation differences. Because there are thousands of words in English with Latin roots, "making the cognate connection" is an important skill for ELLs to acquire.

Implications for High-Stakes Testing

For Spanish speakers, recognizing cognates is a powerful tool for understanding the academic vocabulary on high-stakes tests. However, the key is that commonly used, high-frequency Spanish words have English cognates that are much more academic in nature. These English academic words are not used frequently in conversational English, but do appear regularly in texts.

For example, *determinar* is a Spanish high-frequency word. The English cognate is *determine*. *Determine* is more likely to be found in the academic language used in a textbook. In speech, we would say *decide*. See the following table for additional examples.

Table 2.3: Additional Cognate Examples

Spanish	Academic English	Conversational English
Mathematics		
error	error	mistake
determinar	determine	decide
velocidad	velocity	speed
Science		
subterráneo	subterranean	underground
olfato	olfaction	smell
mandibula	mandibles	jaw

Spanish	Academic English	Conversational English
Social Studies		
elegir	elect	choose
tarifa	tariff	fee
colegas	colleagues	coworkers
Language Arts		
encontrar	encounter	find
significar	to signify	to mean
amigable	amicable	friendly

Lesson Plan for Spanish and English Cognates

Materials

- The Cognate Restaurant (page 55), one per student

- El Restaurante de los Cognados (page 56), one per student

- Science Cognates list (pages 57–59), one copy per student

- Mathematics Cognates list (pages 60–61), one copy per student

- False Cognates handout (page 62), one per student

- Realia (cereal box, chocolate, banana, tea bag, coffee, tomato soup can)

- Dictionaries, one per group

- Science textbooks, one per student

- Newspapers and magazines, one copy per group

- State or provincial assessment passages, one copy per group

- Transparency of a selected passage from the science textbook

Activities

1. Tell students that they already have a tool that they can use to be better readers and writers of English. They have the ability to use this tool because they are Spanish speakers.

2. Hold up the realia, piece by piece, and ask the students what each one is. Write the English and Spanish names of the items on the board or overhead as you hold them up (see El Restaurante de los Cognados for Spanish translations). Ask students what they notice (that the words are the same or similar in both languages).

3. Distribute one copy of The Cognate Restaurant to each student. Ask them, **If your parents or someone you know who cannot speak any English saw this menu in a restaurant, would they be able to understand it?** Distribute one copy of El Restaurante de los Cognados to each student. Have them look at the Spanish side of the menu, and compare the two sides. Ask students what they notice.

4. Provide each student with a copy of the Science Cognates list. Read through the words together, and ask the students what they notice. Explain to students that words with the same or similar spelling and also the same meaning are called cognates. There are more than 7,000 Spanish/English cognates. After students learn how to "make the cognate connection," they will have a larger vocabulary and will be able to predict the meanings of unknown words.

5. Brainstorm a list of cognates that students know that are not on the list (animals are a good topic for this).

6. Have students open their science textbooks to a familiar passage. Using a transparency copy of the passage, read through it together, stopping to identify and underline cognates, and have students look the cognates up in the dictionary. As cognates are found, write them on the board. Discuss the variations between English and Spanish in the spelling patterns of the prefixes and suffixes.

7. Have students pair up and read through newspaper or magazine articles and find cognates, underlining them and making a list on a separate piece of paper.

8. In the same pairs, have students read through a copy of a passage from a state or provincial assessment, underlining the cognates and writing the equivalent Spanish word in the margin. As a culminating activity, read through the passage with the students and identify the cognates, allowing students to modify their notations as needed. Help students understand the use of cognates to determine word meanings.

9. In these explorations, students may discover that some words that seem to be cognates do not mean the same thing. If students do not realize this concept, present examples to illustrate it. Explain that there are "false" cognates but that only one of every ten cognates is false. Give a copy of the False Cognates handout to each student.

Greek and Latin Word Parts List

Greek Roots	Latin Roots
Prefixes	**Prefixes**
ante- = before	aqua- = water
anthrop- = man	aud- = hear, listen to
anti- = against	cap- = take, hold
aster- (astro) = star	contra- = against
auto- = self	cred- = believe
biblio- = book	de- = down from, reverse
bio- = life	dict- = tell, speak
dem- = people	fac- = make, do
derm- = skin	fort- = strong
gam- = marriage	gen- = race, birth, type
geo- = earth	inter- = between
mal- = badly	man-, manu- = hand
micro- = small	met-, miss- = send, sent
mis- = wrongly	mis- = wrong, incorrect
miso- = hatred	non- = not
phil- = love	ped-, pod- = foot
post- = after	port- = carry
pseudo- = false	post- = after
psych- = mind	re- = again
tele- = far	spec(t)- = look
zo- = animal	trans- = across
Suffixes	tri- = three
-crat, -cracy = power, rule	via-, vis- = see
-graph, -gram = writing, record	voc- = call
-ism = action, condition	
-ist = person	
-ology = study of	
-path = feeling, disease	
-phobe, -phobia = fear	
-phone = sound	
-phile = loving	
-scope = sight	

Question Cards

Why is a *microscope* called a microscope?	How does a *microscope* differ from a *telescope*?
How does a *telephone* differ from a *telegram*?	What is the purpose of *antifreeze* in an automobile engine?
What happens if something *malfunctions*?	What is the difference between a *postdated* check and an *antedated* check?
If *a-* means without, what does *apolitical* mean?	If *biology* is the study of life, what is *anthropology*?

continued

Teaching Your Secondary ELLs the Academic Language of Tests: Focusing on Language in Mathematics, Science, and Social Studies
© 2009 r4 Educated Solutions • solution-tree.com • Visit **go.solution-tree.com/ELL** to download this page.

Question Cards (continued)

What is *astrology*?	What is a *philanthropist*?
What word means the study of animals?	If *geo-* means earth, what does *geology* mean?
If you have an *auditory* problem, what kind of problem do you have?	What do the word parts in *democracy* mean?
If you contradict someone's *hypothesis*, what are you doing?	Would you like to be called a *bibliophile*? Why or why not?

continued

Question Cards (continued)

If you did not know what *manufacture* means, how could you figure it out?	If *edible* means something that can be eaten, what does *inedible* mean?
What root do *pedal* and *pedestrian* have in common, and what does it mean?	When you give *credence* to someone's story, what are you doing?
If *tri-* means three, what is a *triangle*?	

Word Web

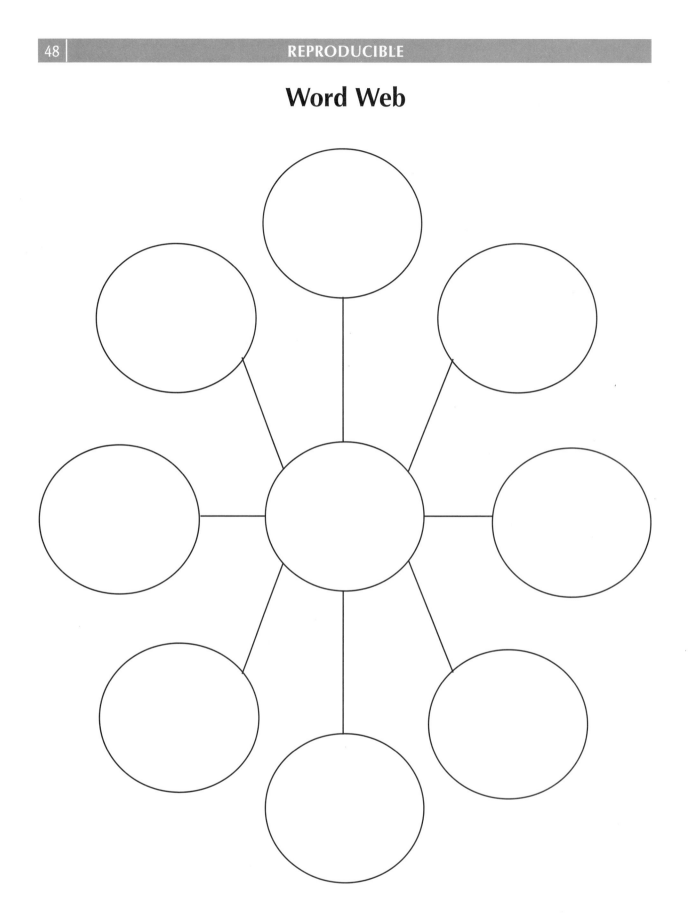

Word Parts Scavenger Hunt

Name: _____

Date: _____

Word Part	Word From Textbook	Context in Which Word Is Used	Predicted Definition	Glossary Definition

Lab Report

Student Name(s): _____   Date: _____

Title: _____
Be brief and concise, yet descriptive.

Statement of the Problem

What question(s) are you trying to answer? Include any preliminary observations or background information about the subject.

_____

_____

_____

Hypothesis

Write a possible solution for the problem. Make sure the solution is testable.

_____

_____

_____

Materials

Make a list of ALL items used in the lab.

_____   _____

_____   _____

_____   _____

Procedure

Explain what you did in the lab. The procedure should be written so that anyone could repeat the experiment.

_____

_____

_____

_____

continued

Teaching Your Secondary ELLs the Academic Language of Tests: Focusing on Language in Mathematics, Science, and Social Studies
© 2009 r4 Educated Solutions • solution-tree.com • Visit **go.solution-tree.com/ELL** to download this page.

Results (Data)

Include any data tables, observations, or additional notes you make during the lab, including tables, graphs, or charts.

_____

_____

_____

_____

Analysis

Draw inferences about what you have learned.

_____

_____

_____

_____

Conclusions

- Accept or reject your hypothesis.

- Explain why you accepted or rejected your hypothesis using data from the lab.

- Include a summary of the data (averages, highest, lowest, and so on) to help the reader understand your results.

- List one thing you learned and describe how it applies to a real-life situation.

- Discuss possible errors that could have occurred (experimental errors) in the collection of the data.

_____

_____

_____

_____

_____

Sample Science Question With Graphic

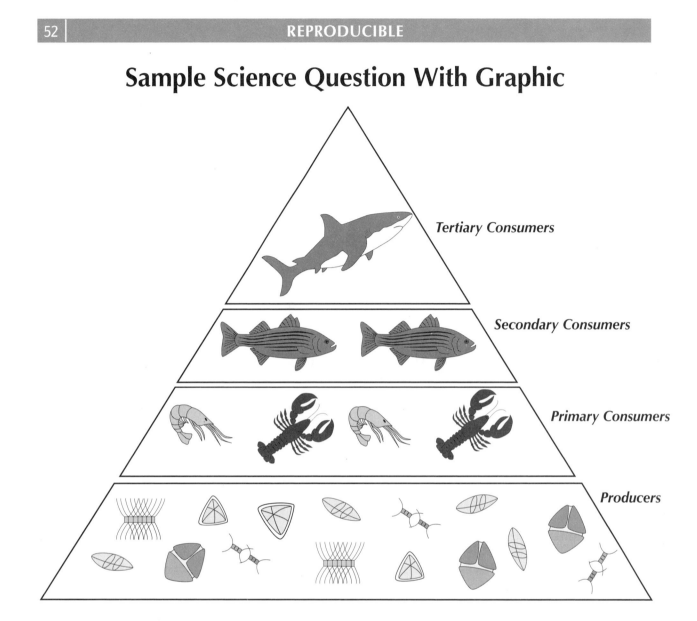

1. The difference in the size of each level of this food pyramid represents the result of the difference in:

    A. The food that individual niches choose

    B. The ocean areas of habitat

    C. The amount of available energy at each level

    D. The size of the organisms

Sample Signal Words

accordingly	may be due to
after	meanwhile
afterward	next
as a result of	not long after
as soon as	now
because	on (date)
before	preceding
begins with	prior
consequently	second
during	so that
finally	soon
first	steps involved
following	then
for this reason	therefore
if . . . then	third
immediately	thus
in order to	today
initially	when
is/was caused by	while
last	until
later	yesterday
leads/led to	

Footprints

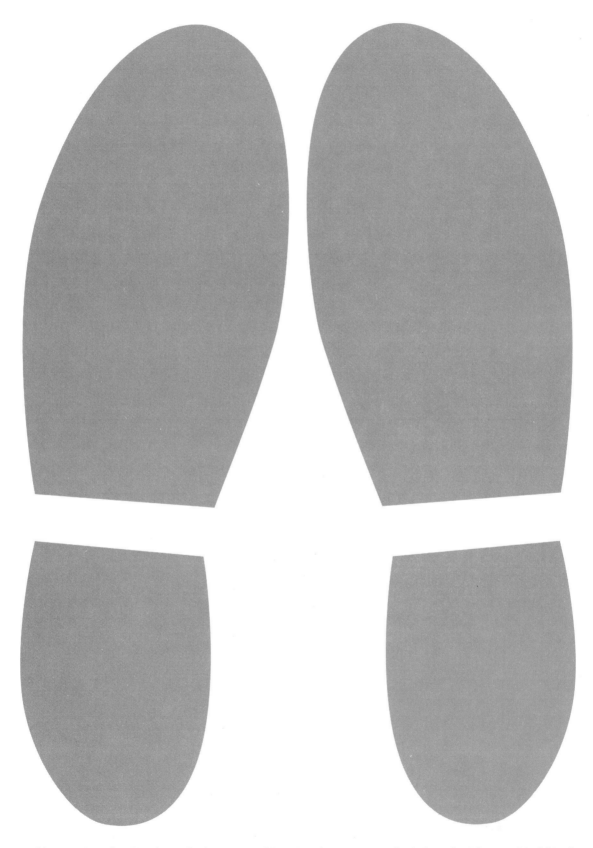

The Cognate Restaurant

Breakfast

Cereal

Toast

Banana

Coffee

Tea

Lunch

Sandwich

Fruit Salad

Tomato Soup

Soda

Dinner

Steak

Potato

Salad

Cauliflower

Chocolate Tart

El Restaurante de los Cognados

Desayuno

Cereal

Pan tostado

Banana

Café

Té

Almuerzo

Sándwich

Ensalada de fruta

Sopa de tomate

Soda

Cena

Bistec

Patata

Ensalada

Coliflor

Tarta de chocolate

Science Cognates

actividad volcánica	volcanic activity	conclusiones	conclusions
analice	analyze	consistencia	consistency
apropiada	appropriate	constancia	constancy
asteroides	asteroids	constantemente	constantly
atmósfera	atmosphere	consumidores	consumers
átomos	atoms	continental	continental
axis	axis	contribuciones	contributions
balanzas	balances	crítico	critical
biomasa	biomass	decisiones	decisions
calculadores	calculators	defina	define
calidad del aire	air quality	describa	describe
cambios graduales	gradual changes	descubrimientos	discoveries
catastrófico	catastrophic	día	day
células	cells	dirección	direction
ciclo	cycle	directo(a)	direct
ciclo del agua	water cycle	distribuye	distribute
ciclo del carbono	carbon cycle	dominante	dominant
ciclo de la roca	rock cycle	ecosistema	ecosystem
ciencia	science	eléctrico(a)	electrical
científicos	scientists	endotérmico(a)	endothermic
ciertos tipos	certain types	energía	energy
cilindros graduados	graduated cylinders	energía cinética	kinetic energy
clasifique	classify	energía potencial	potential energy
cometas	comets	energía radiante	radiant energy
compases	compasses	equilibrio	equilibrium
compleja	complex	equipo	equipment
componentes	components	espacio	space
compuestos	composed	especies	species
computadores	computers	estímulos	stimuli
comunique	communicate	estructura(s)	structure(s)
conceptos	concepts	evalúe	evaluate
conceptual	conceptual	eventos	events
conservación	conservation	evidencia	evidence

continued

Science Cognates (continued)

examine	examine	información	information
exotérmico(a)	exothermic	informadas	informed
explicaciones	explanations	instrumentos	instruments
explique	explain	interacciones	interactions
externos	external	interdependencia	interdependence
extinción	extinction	interno(a)	internal
extrapole	extrapolate	interprete	interpret
fases	phases	laboratorio	laboratory
fenómeno	phenomenon	limitaciones	limitations
fiebre	fever	mapas	maps
formule	formulate	máquinas simples	simple machines
formulas	formulas	matemático	mathematical
frecuencia	frequency	materia	matter
fuerza	force	material(es)	material(s)
función	function	meteoritos	meteorites
galaxia	galaxy	métodos	methods
generaciones	generations	metros	meters
genético(a)	genetic	microscopios	microscopes
gráficamente	graphically	movimiento	movement
gráficas	graphics	natural	natural
herencia	inheritance	nitrógeno	nitrogen
hidroeléctrico(a)	hydroelectric	no renovable	nonrenewable
hipótesis	hypothesis	observaciones	observations
historia	history	observe	observe
humano(a)	human	obtengaocéano	obtain
huracanes	hurricanes	océano	ocean
identifique	identify	órbita	orbit
impacto	impact	organismos	organisms
inagotable	inexhaustible	organice	organize
incluyendo	including	órganos	organs
indirecta	indirect	origen	origin
individual	individual	originales	original
inferencias	inferences	oxígeno	oxygen

continued

Science Cognates (continued)

partes	parts	sociedad	society
planetas	planets	solución	solution
plantas	plants	substancias	substances
plásticos	plastics	sucesión ecológica	ecological
porcentaje	percent	superficie	surface
posición	position	sustentas	sustain
prácticas éticas	ethical practices	tabla periódica	periodic table
presencia	presence	tablas	tables
problema	problem	telescopios	telescopes
producción	production	teorías	theories
propiedades	chemical properties	términos	terms
razonables	reasonable	termómetro	thermometer
recesivo(a)	recessive	tipos	types
reciclaje	recycling	transformaciones	transformations
recomendaciones	recommendations	transforme	transform
renovable	renewable	tubos	tubes
represente	represent	universo	universe
reproducción sexual	sexual reproduction	válido(a)	valid
rotación	rotation	vapor de agua	water vapor
sistema solar	solar system	variedad(es)	variety(ies)
sistemas	systems	volcán	volcano
sistemas de órganos	organ systems	vomitar	vomiting

Mathematics Cognates

actividades	activities	división	division
algebraico	algebraic	ecuación	equation
analice	analyze	equivalente	equivalent
ángulos	angles	espacial	spatial
aplica	applies	estadísticas	statistics
aplicación	application	estimación	estimation
área	area	estime	estimate
arquitectura	architecture	evalúe	evaluate
arte	art	evento simple	simple event
capacidad	capacity	exacto(a)	exact
cilindros	cylinders	experiencias	experiences
círculo	circle	experimental	experimental
circunferencia	circumference	exponentes	exponents
comunes	common	factores	factors
compare	compare	factorizaciones	factorizations
complementario	complementary	físicos	physics
complemento	complement	formas	forms
conclusiones	conclusions	fórmulas	formulas
concreto(a)	concrete	fracciones	fractions
conos	cones	genere	generate
conversiones	conversions	geometría	geometry
convierta	convert	geométrico	geometric
coordenada	coordinate	incorpore	incorporate
cuadriláteros	quadrilaterals	informal	informal
cuantitativo	quantitative	interpretando	interpreting
cuantitativo razonamiento	quantitative reasoning	investigaciones	investigations
decimales	decimals	lenguaje	language
decisiones	decisions	lógico(a)	logical
densidad	density	matemática	mathematics
describa	describe	modelos	models
diámetro	diameter	modelos concretos	concrete models
dimensiones	dimensions	modelos geométricos	geometric models
disciplinas	disciplines	modo	mode

continued

Teaching Your Secondary ELLs the Academic Language of Tests: Focusing on Language in Mathematics, Science, and Social Studies
© 2009 r4 Educated Solutions • solution-tree.com • Visit go.solution-tree.com/ELL to download this page.

Mathematics Cognates (continued)

multiplicación	multiplication		radio	radius
múltiplos	multiples		rango	range
no negativos	non-negative		razonable	reasonable
nombra	name		razonamiento	reasoning
números	numbers		redondee	round
objetos	objects		relaciones	relationships
obtuso(a)	obtuse		representaciones	representations
operaciones	operations		represente	represent
ordene	order		resultados	results
organizando	organizing		secuencias	sequences
papel	paper		símbolos	symbols
pares ordenados	ordered pairs		sistemáticamente	systematically
patrones	patterns		situaciones	situations
pentágonos	pentagons		solución	solution
perímetro	perimeter		suplementario	supplementary
pirámides	pyramids		tablas	tables
plan	plan		técnicas	techniques
polígonos	polygons		tecnología	technology
porcentajes	percentages		temperatura	temperature
precio	price		teorema de Pitágoras	Pythagorean Theorem
predicciones	predictions		teoría	theory
prismas	prisms		triángulos	triangles
probabilidad(es)	probability(ies)		unidades	units
problemas	problems		unidades apropiadas	appropriate units
procesos	processes		valide	validate
propiedades	properties		variedad	variety
proporcional	proportional		vocabulario	vocabulary
proporcionalidad	proportionality		volumen de un prisma rectangular	volume of a rectangular prism
puntos	points			
racional	rational			

False Cognates

English Word	English Meaning	Spanish Word	Spanish Meaning
actual	real	actual	current, at the present time
assist	assist, help	asistir	to attend
attend	be present	atender	to take care of
billion	1,000,000,000	billón	1,000,000,000,000
bizarre	weird	bizarro	brave
body	physique	boda	wedding
camp	outdoor site	campo	field or countryside
carpet	rug	carpeta	file folder
complexion	coloring of the face	complexión	physiological build
compromise	settle	compromiso	promise or obligation
contest	challenge	contestar	to answer
deception	trickery	decepción	disappointment
delight	enjoyment	delito	crime
disgrace	dishonor	desgracia	mistake
embarrassed	humiliated	embarazada	pregnant
exit	outlet	éxito	hit or success
fabric	cloth	fábrica	factory
football	American game	fútbol	soccer
gang	group	ganga	bargain
large	big	largo	long
once	one time	once	eleven
pretend	fake	pretender	to try
record	write down	recordár	to remember
rope	cord	ropa	clothing
revolver	gun	revolver	to stir
sensible	realistic	sensible	sensitive
soap	cleansing	sopa	soup
success	accomplishment	suceso	event or happening
tuna	fish	tuna	cactus or glee club

Chapter 3

The Language of Social Studies

Cause and Effect

Social studies texts are often written in expository mode, and their varied sentence structure makes it difficult for English language learners to determine cause and effect. Though cause and effect statements are common, ELLs often interpret the first event in the sentence as occurring first, and the second event in the sentence as occurring later. They fail to recognize key transitions necessary to determine cause and effect.

Implications for High-Stakes Testing

Understanding cause and effect and the sentence structures used to express cause and effect is essential for understanding the texts used on high-stakes tests.

Lesson Plan for Cause and Effect
Materials
• Cause and Effect T-Chart handout (page 77), one per group
• *If You Give a Mouse a Cookie,* by Laura Joffe Numeroff
• Markers, one per group
• Sentence strips, two per group
• Social studies textbook, one per student
• Social studies questions from a state or provincial assessment, one per group

Activities

1. Read *If You Give a Mouse a Cookie* by Laura Joffee Numeroff (or any other children's book with cause-and-effect features) to the students. Start by reading the first few pages; then stop and ask students if they notice a pattern. Continue reading the story, and have students make predictions about what will happen next.

2. Explain that in sentences such as **If you eat all your dinner, then you can get dessert,** the first part of the sentence tells something that might happen. **This is called the cause. It is something that makes something else happen. Out of two events, it is the event that happens first. The second part of the sentence tells what will happen if the first thing happens. This is called the** *effect*. **The effect is what happens because of the cause. Of the two events, it is the one that happens last.**

3. Ask students to think back to the story to determine cause-and-effect events in the story. Discuss this as a whole group.

Cause	Effect
If you give a mouse a cookie	he's going to ask for a glass of milk
When you give him the milk	he'll probably ask you for a straw
When he's finished	he'll ask for a napkin

As examples are discussed, be sure the students understand that the cause is responsible for creating the effect.

4. Ask students to form pairs and think of everyday examples of cause and effect (for example, "I didn't study for my test, so I didn't make a good grade"). Distribute the Cause and Effect T-Chart handout, and have student pairs put their cause statements on one side, and their effect statements on the other. Have students share their statements with the whole group.

5. Tell the students that when determining cause and effect, order is very important. Write the following sentences on the board:

   - If I want a good grade, then I need to study hard.
   - I want a good grade, so I need to study hard.
   - I need to study hard because I want a good grade.

6. Ask students to identify the cause and effect in each sentence. Although the order is inverted in the last sentence, the cause and effect remain the same. **When we use cause**

and effect in speech, we generally use the *if . . . then* transition pattern or the *. . . so . . .* transition pattern. However, other words or phrases can be used to express cause-and-effect transitions. These transition words include the following:

as a result	contributed to	lead to
because	due to	resulted from
because of	effects of	since
by	for	so
cause of	for this reason	so that
consequently	if . . . then	therefore

7. Write these words on the board for students to copy into their notes. Explain that transition words are critical to understanding the cause and the effect in text. With the students, brainstorm examples of sentences using each of the transition words or phrases listed. Write the sentences on the board.

8. Have students go back to their pairs and the Cause and Effect T-Charts they created in Step 4. Using the examples from the story, show students how to write each cause-and-effect sentence in the inverted form. Write the reverse-order sentence on the board.

Original Sentence	Inverted Sentence
If you give a mouse a cookie, he's probably going to ask for a glass of milk.	A mouse will probably ask for a glass of milk if you give him a cookie.
When you give him the milk, he'll probably ask you for a straw.	He'll probably ask you for a straw because you gave him the milk.
When he's finished, he'll ask for a napkin.	He'll ask for a napkin because he's finished.

Now have the students select an example sentence from their T-Charts and write the sentence on a sentence strip. On a second sentence strip, have the students write the reverse-order sentence. Have students share their second inverted sentences with the whole group, and let the class determine the cause and the effect.

9. Instruct students to look in their social studies textbooks and at sample social studies questions from a state or provincial assessment for examples of cause and effect using the previous patterns and transitions.

Chronology

Social studies texts are often written in expository mode, and their varied sentence structure makes it difficult for English language learners to construct events in chronological order. Often, ELLs list events in the order related in the sentence instead of in the order of actual occurrence. They fail to recognize key "time" words that are imperative for understanding chronology of events.

Implications for High-Stakes Testing

As students understand that events do not necessarily occur in the order related in a sentence or text, as well as understand the relationship of time words to events in the sentence or text, they will be better able to determine chronology.

Lesson Plan for Chronology

Materials

- Sequence Cards (page 79), one set per group

- Sequence Picture Cards (page 78) or short comic strips, one per group

- Sentence strips, four per group

- Markers, one per group

- Social studies textbook, one per student

- Social studies questions from a state or provincial assessment, one per student

Activities

1. Form groups of two to four students.

2. Give groups a set of the Sequence Picture Cards or four panels from a short comic strip, cut apart. Ask the students to place the pictures in chronological order or in the sequence in which they occur. Have students explain why they placed the cards in this order; then have them write a sentence for each picture on a sentence strip. Have students put them in chronological order under the pictures.

3. Explain to students that just as the pictures give clues to the order in which things occur, so do specific words.

---

4. Give each group a set of the Sequence Cards, and have them put these cards in front of the appropriate picture and sentence. Then ask the students to read their sentences using these "time" words. (For example, "First, an acorn is planted. Second, a sprout begins to grow. Third, a sapling grows stronger. Fourth, the tree matures.").

5. Ask the students to brainstorm other words or phrases that show time or chronology and put them on sentence strips. Ask students to create sentences using these words with their Picture Cards and original sentences. (Examples might include *to begin*, *next*, *after that*, *finally*, and so on. Students will usually come up with linear words that maintain sequential order.)

6. Change the order of the original sentences; for example, "The tree matures. A sprout begins to grow. An acorn is planted. A sapling grows stronger." Explain to students that for this example to make sense, additional words and/or phrases must be added so that the order of events is clear. At this point, model a sentence such as "Before an oak tree can grow into a mature tree, an acorn must be planted." Explain that the word *before* shows when something happens in relation to another event. The order of events (pictures) does not change, but the order of the sentences does change.

7. Depending on students' proficiency level, either have them brainstorm or give them additional words or phrases that show time or chronology. Ask students to use them to modify their original sentences, noting how the words change the order of the sentence strips but do not actually change the order in which the events occur.

8. After students have had the opportunity to manipulate the sentences within their group and share with the whole group for practice and clarification, ask students to look at a paragraph or page in their social studies text, searching for these words or phrases that show chronological order. If students need additional support, ask them to draw pictures of the events in order to manipulate and place them in the correct order. Have students share with the whole group. Make sure that they take notes of the words or phrases as well as the order of events.

9. For specific test preparation, review the stems from the state or provincial assessment or other source, noting the words or phrases used in the stems and answer choices that show time. Again, drawing pictures is helpful.

10. For reinforcement, continue to point out time words or phrases throughout the lessons.

11. For an extension activity, pictures can be placed on a timeline, and students can write a paragraph identifying the order of events.

Multiple Tenses

The text structure of most social studies textbooks includes various and complex verb tense forms. This is often confusing for English language learners who must understand the text structure in order to understand the relationships being studied.

Implications for High-Stakes Testing

Students must be able to understand text structure and tense forms in order to comprehend the relationships, generalizations, and events in social studies. Without knowledge of this structure, students face great obstacles in understanding the social studies concepts assessed.

Lesson Plan for Multiple Tenses

Materials

- Implications of Human-Environment Interaction (page 80), one per student

- Implications of Human-Environment Interaction: Teacher Key (page 81)

- Sentence strips, one package

- Red and green overhead markers

- Implications of Human-Environment Interaction, copied onto a transparency

- Social studies textbook, one per student

Activities

1. Write your name on the board. Ask the students to think of as many statements as they can to tell about you. Allow both general (*Mrs. Barry is nice*) and specific (*Mrs. Barry was born in Houston*) statements. As students provide statements, write them on sentence strips.

2. Put the sentence strips together to form a paragraph. Read the paragraph aloud to the students.

3. Ask students to divide the statements into those that are general statements and those that are specific. Ask the students if they notice anything about the verbs in each category. (Students should be able to cite verb phrases, specifically past and present tense, even if they are unfamiliar with the actual terms related to verb forms.) Point out to students that sometimes present and past tenses are used in the same paragraph. In social studies textbooks, the general statements made are often written in the present tense, and the specific statements are often written in the past tense.

---

4. Remind students that all the statements they provided about you are related to the same person and can be arranged in one paragraph, even though some are general and written in the present tense, and some are specific and written in the past tense. Explain that in social studies texts, present tense is usually used for making general statements, and past tense is generally used for specific events.

5. Display the transparency of Implications of Human-Environment Interaction on an overhead projector. Distribute a copy of the Implications of Human-Environment Interaction handout to each student. Read the first section "Hurricane Origins" and have students follow along. In a whole-group discussion, review the events in the passage and identify each event as a general or specific statement. As each statement is identified, underline general statements in the present tense with a red overhead marker once and specific statements in the past tense with a green overhead marker twice. Circle the verb or verbs in each statement that identify each statement as present or past tense. Review and discuss the answers.

6. Ask students to read silently the second section, "High Winds and Surge," and identify the general and specific statements in the passage. Instruct students to underline general statements in the present tense once and specific statements in the past tense twice. Have students circle the verb(s) in each statement that helps identify each statement as present or past tense. Review and discuss the answers.

7. Divide students into groups of two or four. Instruct each group to search in their social studies textbook for paragraph(s) similar to the paragraphs presented on the transparency. Have each group rewrite the paragraph they found in their textbook using the sentence strips, writing one sentence per sentence strip. Ask each group to categorize the sentences into general or specific statements, and circle the verb or verbs that help(s) identify each statement as present or past tense. Review and discuss group findings.

8. Have students continue to practice when reading their social studies textbooks.

Pronouns

The use of pronouns in social studies texts often confuses English language learners who fail to comprehend the antecedents. This leads to misunderstanding and lack of success.

Implications for High-Stakes Testing

If students are not able to understand pronoun-antecedent agreement, they will be unable to grasp basic social studies skills and concepts.

Lesson Plan for Pronouns

Materials

- Pronoun List chart (page 82), one chart per student
- Pronoun Practice Passages handout (pages 83–84), one per student
- Transparency of Pronoun Practice Passages
- Transparency of Pronoun List
- Map pencils or markers, various colors, one set per student
- Overhead markers, various colors

Activities

1. Review pronouns with students, reminding them that pronouns take the place of nouns. Distribute a copy of the Pronoun List chart to each student. Display the transparency of the Pronoun List chart on an overhead projector.

2. Explain that a subject pronoun is the subject of the sentence and that it takes the place of the noun. For example:

   Juan lives in Houston.

   <u>He</u> lives in Houston. The pronoun *he* takes the place of *Juan.*

3. Explain that an object pronoun is the object of the verb in the sentence and that it takes the place of the noun. For example:

   Give Monica the book.

   Give <u>her</u> the book. The pronoun *her* takes the place of *Monica.*

4. Explain that a possessive pronoun shows that something belongs to someone. For example:

   That book belongs to Kristy.

   That book is <u>hers</u>. The pronoun *hers* shows that the book belongs to Kristy.

5. As a whole group, discuss the pronouns and have the students share examples of their usage.

6. Pair students and give each student a copy of the Pronoun Practice Passages handout.

7. Display a transparency of Pronoun Practice Passage 1 on an overhead projector, and direct the students' attention to Passage 1 on their Pronoun Practice Passages hand-out. Have the students read the passage silently as you read the passage aloud. Explain that this passage is representative of those found in social studies texts.

8. Explain to students that pronouns are used to simplify a sentence, reduce repetition, and make a sentence sound more natural. Then, with an overhead marker, underline the proper noun *George H. W. Bush* with one color each time it appears in Passage 1. Have students do the same with a map pencil or marker. (See Answer Key, Part I, page 72.)

9. Ask students to identify pronouns from the Pronoun List that could be used in place of the proper noun *George H. W. Bush*. Using the first sentence in Passage 1, explain to students that you can use a pronoun to replace the second mention of *George H. W. Bush* to reduce repetition. Explain that this is helpful to readers because *George H. W. Bush* has already been identified as the subject in the beginning of the sentence. The third and fourth time it appears, cross out the name, and replace it with a pronoun. (See Answer Key, Part II, page 72.)

10. Ask students to underline all incidents of *Iraq* using a different color map pencil or marker. Do the same to Passage 1, using a different color overhead marker. (See Answer Key, Part I, page 72.) Next, have students cross out the proper noun *Iraq* each time it is repeated in the passage. Do the same to Passage 1. Ask each student pair to come up with a pronoun to replace the crossed-out words. (See Answer Key, Part II, page 72.) Facilitate this process by moving among the pairs, offering assistance when needed.

11. Ask the students if they can locate any other nouns that could be replaced with pronouns from the Pronoun List. Have pairs complete this activity using a third color for any nouns they find. Use the Answer Key on page 72 to review answers with students.

12. Ask students to read Passage 2. Have the students underline each different noun in a different color. Have them cross out the second and subsequent mentions of each noun and replace them with pronouns, where appropriate, using the same color for the noun and its replacement. Review corrections with students before continuing.

13. Explain to students that the *antecedent* is the word that the pronoun represents. Ask students to read Passage 3. Ask student volunteers to come to the overhead and underline each pronoun found in the passage. Ask students to identify the antecedent(s) of each pronoun by writing the antecedent above the pronoun it represents. After students have completed the passage, discuss the activity with group members and ask them to explain how they determined which antecedent each pronoun referred to.

14. Ask students to read Passage 4. With their partners, have students underline each pronoun found in the passage and identify the antecedent(s) of each pronoun by writing the antecedent above the pronoun it represents.

Answer Key

Part I

When <u>George H. W. Bush</u> won the presidency in 1988, people believed that <u>George H. W. Bush</u> would continue in the same manner as <u>George H. W. Bush's</u> predecessor, President Ronald Reagan. For the first two years of <u>George H. W. Bush's</u> presidency, the situation proved to be true. Then in August, 1990, <u>Iraq</u> invaded a small country on <u>Iraq's</u> southern border, Kuwait, in order to control the oil supplies there. Under the rule of <u>Saddam Hussein</u>, <u>Iraq</u> had been involved in a long-lasting, expensive war with <u>Iraq's</u> neighbor to the east, Iran. <u>Saddam Hussein</u> needed to replenish <u>Iraq's</u> treasure. <u>Saddam Hussein</u> believed that oil revenues from Kuwait, a small monarch with one of the highest per-capita incomes in the world, would do this.

Part II

When <u>George H. W. Bush</u> won the presidency in 1988, people believed *he* <s>George H. W.</s>

<s>Bush</s> would continue in the same manner as <s>George H. W. Bush's</s> *his* predecessor,

President Ronald Reagan. For the first two years of <s>George H. W. Bush's</s> *his* presidency, the

situation proved to be true. Then in August, 1990, <u>Iraq</u> invaded a small country on

<s>Iraq's</s> *its* southern border, Kuwait, in order to control the oil supplies there. Under the rule

of <u>Saddam Hussein</u>, <s>Iraq</s> *it* had been involved in a long-lasting, expensive war with <s>Iraq's</s> *its*

neighbor to the east, Iran. <s>Saddam Hussein</s> *He* needed to replenish <s>Saddam Hussein's</s> *his*

country's treasure. <s>Saddam Hussein</s> *He* believed that oil revenues from Kuwait, a small

monarch with one of the highest per-capita incomes in the world, would do this.

Multiple-Meaning Words

One of the most difficult aspects of English is that it contains many words that can have multiple meanings and also be more than one part of speech. These words are often used in multiple subject areas in different contexts. Students must be able to determine meaning in order to successfully negotiate concepts in various subject areas.

Implications for High-Stakes Testing

To fully understand the concepts being assessed, students must have strategies to determine the contextually appropriate meaning for multiple-meaning words.

Lesson Plan for Multiple-Meaning Words

Materials

- Multiple-Meaning Words Chart handout (page 85), one per student

- Blank paper, two sheets per student

- Markers, one set per student

- Stapler

Activities

1. Write the following statements on the board. Ask students to do a think-pair-share to discuss how the meaning of the word *cool* differs in each sentence.

    - **The fan will cool me off.**

    - **The new Fall Out Boy album is cool!**

2. Explain that in different contexts, words in English can have different meanings and can be used as different parts of speech when used in different contexts. It is important to consider the context of a word before deciding on a meaning.

3. Have students place their top sheet of paper one inch above the bottom edge of the second sheet (see figure 3.1).

4. Fold the set of papers so that the top sheet is one inch above its bottom edge (see figure 3.2 on page 74). This will create a flip book. Staple the book along the fold.

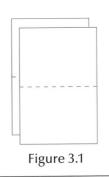

Figure 3.1

5. On the top flap, ask students to write the word *Table* (see figure 3.3). Explain that *table* is a word in English that has multiple meanings.

6. On the second flap, on the bottom edge, ask students to write the part of speech (noun). Ask them to write the following definition: *A piece of furniture.* (See figure 3.4.)

7. Raise the top flap, and ask the students to draw a picture of a table on this section. Ask them to write the following sentence (or a sentence of their own creation) on the top of the page: *I sat at the table to eat dinner.* (See figure 3.5.)

8. On the third flap, on the next edge, ask students to write the part of speech (*noun*) and definition of the word *table: A list of numbers, facts, or information arranged in rows across and down on a page.* As before, ask students to draw a picture representing this definition, and copy the following sentence (or a sentence of their own creation): *The table shows the amount of rain that fell during each month.* Instruct students to write their sentences at the top of the page, leaving enough room to add more information. (See figure 3.6.)

9. On the last flap, on the bottom edge, ask students to write the part of speech (*verb*) and definition of *table: To decide to deal with an offer or idea at a later time.* Once again, ask students to draw a picture representing this definition, and copy the following sentence (or a sentence of their own creation): *The committee decided to table the discussion when it could not agree on a solution to the problem.* Instruct students to write their sentences at the top of the page, leaving enough room to add more information. (See figure 3.7.)

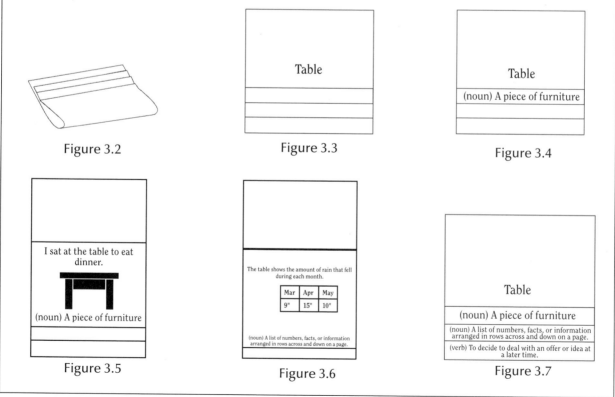

Figure 3.2

Figure 3.3

Figure 3.4

Figure 3.5

Figure 3.6

Figure 3.7

10. Ask students to think of times when these words might be used and in which subject area. Explain that this flip book can be used to help learn vocabulary and determine which definition is appropriate in different contexts.

11. Repeat this strategy for additional multiple-meaning words encountered. Students can use the Multiple-Meaning Words Chart to compile a list of multiple-meaning words they encounter through instruction or their own reading. Some multiple-meaning words that can be used for instruction include the following:

account	draft	pass	solution
act	draw	place	stake
bill	evaluate	plant	stock
capital	fault	rate	table
cell	field	scale	wave
cover	land	set	web

Maps and Charts

The vocabulary used on maps and charts is very specialized. In order to fully comprehend geography and geographical concepts, students must have a firm foundation in the knowledge of these terms.

Implications for High-Stakes Testing

Students must be knowledgeable in both vocabulary and application of geographical terms and concepts in order to successfully master requirements of any social studies assessments.

Lesson Plan for Maps and Charts

Materials

- Vocabulary Word Cards (page 86), one set per group
- Globes, one per group
- Variety of maps for each group (world, continent, state, city, and so on)
- Chart paper, one sheet per group
- Markers, one set per group
- Blank paper, several sheets per student

Activities

1. Form groups of three to four students. Give each group a globe and some relevant maps (of the world, continent, state, or city). Ask students to make a t-chart on their chart paper. Ask, **What is common to all of these items? What is unique to each?** Have groups record answers on a t-chart, labeling one side *Common Attributes* and the other side *Unique Attributes*. Have groups share with the whole class.

2. As groups are sharing, introduce and explain the appropriate vocabulary on the Vocabulary Word Cards to define the commonalities and differences given by students. For example, if the students say that each of the items reviewed has vertical lines, then introduce the concept of latitude. Have the students illustrate the word *latitude* on the back of that word card. Continue until all vocabulary words are addressed. Selected vocabulary should include *latitude, longitude, scale, Prime Meridian, hemisphere, compass rose, north, south, east, west, key, boundaries, landforms, ocean, island, continent*, and any other words associated with grade-level expectations.

3. Ask groups to categorize the words. For example, *latitude, longitude, north, south, east, west*, and *compass rose* could all be placed in a category labeled *Direction Words*. Instead of having predetermined headings, allow students to make their own connections regarding the vocabulary. Once the groups have divided the words into categories, have them explain why they created the groups that they did.

4. To ensure understanding of map skills and vocabulary, ask students to create their own maps of an imaginary country, being sure to include all elements on the vocabulary list.

Cause and Effect T-Chart

Cause Statements	*Effect Statements*

Sequence Picture Cards

Sequence Cards

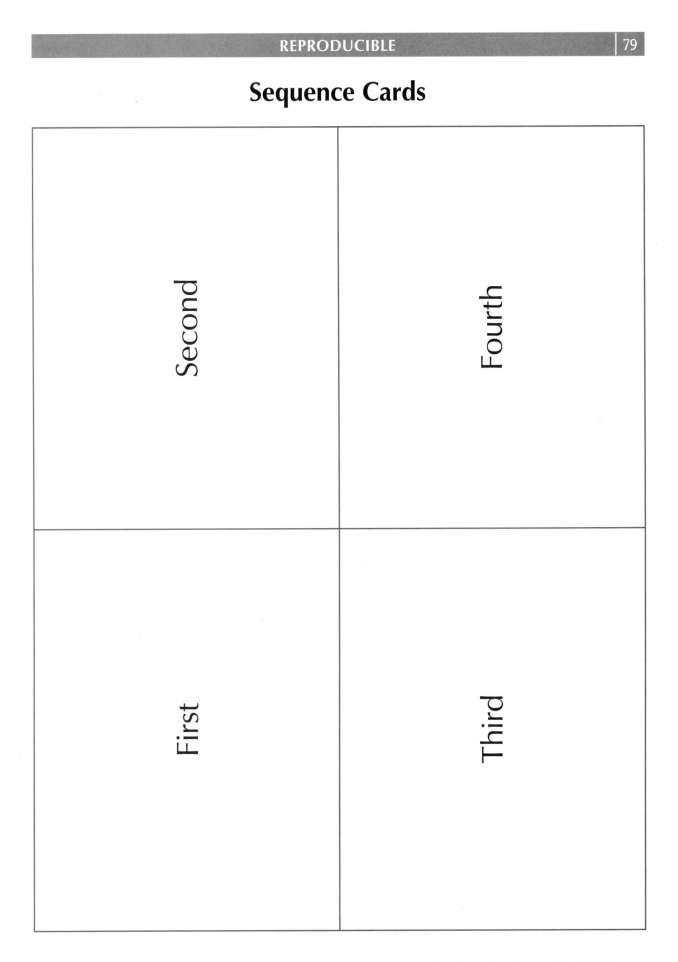

Second

Fourth

First

Third

Implications of Human-Environment Interaction

Hurricane Origins

For the 38,000 inhabitants of Galveston, Texas, September 8, 1900, began the same as any other. While an early morning account of a tropical hurricane in the Gulf of Mexico ran on page three of Galveston's local newspaper, it was little warning for the arrival of Galveston's Great Storm of 1900—one of the deadliest weather disasters in United States history.

Hurricanes originate in tropical or subtropical waters between Africa and the Americas, travel east to west, and typically make landfall along the coastal regions of either the Gulf of Mexico or Atlantic Ocean. Hurricanes are one of the most destructive forces in nature. Galveston's hurricane of 1900 claimed the lives of at least 6,000 people on the southeast Texas coastline, left 10,000 homeless, and destroyed more than 3,600 buildings.

High Winds and Surge

Because hurricane force winds are 100 miles per hour or more, houses along the coastlines of the Gulf of Mexico or Atlantic Ocean typically follow stricter building codes. For example, L-joint brackets secure the studs in the walls to the roof so that the roof is less likely to blow off. Storm shutters protect windows against flying debris.

If a hurricane makes landfall, residents also encounter tidal surge and storm surge. The surge produced by Hurricane Ike in Galveston in September, 2008, flooded homes and buildings on the coastline and in downtown Galveston. In some cases, entire houses on the coastline vanished. In 2005, the surge produced by Hurricane Katrina breached New Orleans' levees, resulting in catastrophic damage to the area.

Despite a hurricane's great potential for damage and loss of life, there are usually no more than a dozen named storms each year. Only three or four hurricanes typically make landfall and cause extensive damage.

Implications of Human-Environment Interaction: Teacher Key

Hurricane Origins

For the 38,000 inhabitants of Galveston, Texas, September 8, 1900, **began** the same as any other. While an early morning account of a tropical hurricane in the Gulf of Mexico **ran** on page three of Galveston's local newspaper, it **was** little warning for the arrival of Galveston's Great Storm of 1900—one of the deadliest weather disasters in United States history.

Hurricanes <u>originate</u> in tropical or subtropical waters between Africa and the Americas, <u>travel</u> east to west, and typically <u>make</u> landfall along the coastal regions of either the Gulf of Mexico or Atlantic Ocean. Hurricanes <u>are</u> one of the most destructive forces in nature. Galveston's hurricane of 1900 **claimed** the lives of at least 6,000 people on the southeast Texas coastline, **left** 10,000 homeless, and **destroyed** more than 3,600 buildings.

High Winds and Surge

Because hurricane force winds <u>are</u> 100 miles per hour or more, houses along the coastlines of the Gulf of Mexico or Atlantic Ocean typically <u>follow</u> stricter building codes. For example, L-joint brackets <u>secure</u> the studs in the walls to the roof so that the roof <u>is</u> less likely to blow off. Storm shutters <u>protect</u> windows against flying debris.

If a hurricane <u>makes</u> landfall, residents also <u>encounter</u> tidal surge and storm surge. The surge **produced** by Hurricane Ike in Galveston in September, 2008, **flooded** homes and buildings on the coastline and in downtown Galveston. In some cases, entire houses on the coastline **vanished**. In 2005, the surge **produced** by Hurricane Katrina **breached** New Orleans' levees, resulting in catastrophic damage to the area.

Despite a hurricane's great potential for damage and loss of life, there <u>are</u> usually no more than a dozen named storms each year. Only three or four hurricanes typically <u>make</u> landfall and <u>cause</u> extensive damage.

Key

- General statements are *italicized*.

- Specific statements are plain.

- Present tense verbs are <u>underlined</u>.

- Past tense verbs are in **bold**.

Pronoun List

Subject Pronoun	Object Pronoun	Possessive Pronoun
I	me	mine
you	you	yours
he	him	his
she	her	hers
it	it	its
we	us	our
they	them	theirs

Pronoun List

Subject Pronoun	Object Pronoun	Possessive Pronoun
I	me	mine
you	you	yours
he	him	his
she	her	hers
it	it	its
we	us	our
they	them	theirs

Pronoun Practice Passages

Passage 1

When George H. W. Bush won the presidency in 1988, people believed that George H. W. Bush would continue in the same manner as George H. W. Bush's predecessor, President Ronald Reagan. For the first two years of George H. W. Bush's presidency, the situation proved to be true. Then in August, 1990, Iraq invaded a small country on Iraq's southern border, Kuwait, in order to control the oil supplies there. Under the rule of Saddam Hussein, Iraq had been involved in a long-lasting, expensive war with Iraq's neighbor to the east, Iran. Saddam Hussein needed to replenish Iraq's treasure. Saddam Hussein believed that oil revenues from Kuwait, a small monarch with one of the highest per-capita incomes in the world, would do this.

Passage 2

A violent abolitionist named John Brown led a raid against the United States arsenal at Harpers Ferry, Virginia. John Brown's plan was to capture guns and distribute the weapons to slaves in the surrounding countryside. John Brown wanted slaves to declare freedom by rising up against and killing slave masters. The United States Army, under the command of Colonel Robert E. Lee, ended the raid by surrounding the arsenal and capturing John Brown. They put him on trial for treason against the United States. John Brown was found guilty and later hanged as punishment for John Brown's crime.

continued

Teaching Your Secondary ELLs the Academic Language of Tests: Focusing on Language in Mathematics, Science, and Social Studies
© 2009 r4 Educated Solutions • solution-tree.com • Visit **go.solution-tree.com/ELL** to download this page.

Pronoun Practice Passages (continued)

Passage 3

In 1832 and 1833, Texas colonists held conventions. They wanted the Mexican government to change the way it ruled the Texas colonists. Stephen F. Austin communicated the colonists' wishes to Mexican authorities in July, 1833. Even though the Mexican Congress took some action on the petition, he was arrested and jailed for almost a year. Santa Anna, elected ruler of Mexico, was in the process of becoming a dictator, and he used military power to implement his plans. He wanted to negate the Constitution of 1824 and reorganize state governments, so he sent troops to Texas to carry out his wishes.

Passage 4

In this beautiful Forest City—for it is beautiful notwithstanding the curse that so long hung over it—there is a street where colored people were allowed to walk only on one side. Not long since an acquaintance of mine, while walking on what had been the forbidden side, was rudely pushed off by a white man and told that she had no right there. She gave him to understand that Sherman's March had made Bull Street as much hers as his. Veils were not allowed to be worn by colored women. After the army came in, they went out with two on—one over the face, the other on the back of the bonnet. Many of the planters have returned to their homes. Some wish to make contracts with their former slaves, but the majority are so unfair in their propositions that the people mistrust them.

Multiple-Meaning Words Chart

Name: _____ Date: _____

Word	Definition 1	Definition 2	Definition 3

Vocabulary Word Cards

landforms	east	hemisphere	latitude
ocean	west	compass rose	longitude
island	key	north	scale
continent	boundaries	south	Prime Meridian

Appendices

Teaching Ideas for the Word Lists

The Word Lists for each content area contain more words than it is possible to teach. Select which words from each list that will be taught, based on the importance of the words to the content area and the students' prior knowledge. It is important to choose a reasonable number of words to teach per week, such as five to twelve, and to explicitly teach the words in a cumulative fashion, reviewing previously taught words prior to introducing new words. Students need to have multiple exposures to the words throughout the year and across content areas.

Following are some suggestions for teaching the words.

Word Walls

Write the words on chart paper or on sentence strips in a pocket chart at the front of the room. Use the word wall as a starting point for discussions, warm-ups, journal entries, and games.

Vocabulary Cards

Have the students make cards with the word and its definition, along with a drawing of what the word represents to them. A sentence using the word could be added.

Vocabulary Notebooks

On notebook paper, have students write the word, its definition, and how the word is used in context. Students could also draw a depiction of the word, write sentences using the word, or find the word in textbooks. Vocabulary notebooks are also a good place to record word families for each word. Pages should be organized alphabetically in the notebook.

Mnemonic Devices

Students can choose key words that sound like the vocabulary word to help them remember the word and draw pictures of the key word interacting with the vocabulary word to reinforce the recollection of the meaning.

Word Games

Games such as Pictionary®, Password, and Jeopardy!® reinforce learning and provide interactive opportunities to promote long-term learning.

Word Art

Students can draw the word so that the letters of the word represent the definition of the word. This is also a form of mnemonics.

Appendix A: Math Academic Word List for English Language Learners

Middle School

Test Directions Vocabulary

above	document*	inaccurate	representation*
according to	drawing	information*	ruler
amount	equation*	mark*	sequence*
answer	explain*	necessary*	set
based on*	expression*	pattern*	should
below	fewer	point of view	shown
bubble	figure*	position*	similar*
closest	fill in	procedure	statement
conclusion*	following	reasonable*	support
consideration*	graph*	reasoning	table
correct*	greatest	record	term*
data*	include*	relationship	valid*
describe*	in order to	represent*	value
determine*	in relation*		

*English and Spanish cognates

Test Question Verbs

believe	decide*	increase*	rent*
build	decrease*	land	sell
buy	design	make	ship
calculate*	dilate*	measure	show
choose	divide*	need	spin
collect*	double*	number*	take up
compare*	draw	pay	time
complete*	employ*	plan*	toss
consider*	exceed*	purchase	translate
contain*	find	record*	travel
continue*	graph*	remain	use*
cost*	include*	remove*	

Test Preposition Vocabulary

about	between	of	to
above	by	on	when
as	during*	over	which
at	in	through	with
below			

*English and Spanish cognates

Content Vocabulary

actual*	design	package*	similar*
amount	desire	payment	slab
annual*	dimensions*	price	spinner
architect*	distance*	probability*	stay
bill	drawing	profitable	surface
capacity*	event*	proportion*	tax
case	greatest *	rate	temperature*
certain*	least	rotation*	tile
closest	maximum*	salary	tip
coin	measure	savings	unshaded
company*	minimum*	scale*	view
concrete*	model*	service*	walkway
content*	monthly	set	weight
cost*	notation*	shade	wheel
defective*	nutrition*	shaded	worth

Grade 9

Test Directions Vocabulary

corresponding*	invalid*	results*
equivalent*	nearest	simplify*
generate*	remaining	solution*
given		

*English and Spanish cognates

Test Question Verbs

attend	enclose	place	shift
built	fill	produce*	store
change	inform*	pump	study
consist*	invest*	raise	survey
correspond*	launch	rate	total*
cover	load	receive*	touch
descend*	lower	result	transform*
disprove	map	rise	value
earn	participate*	shape	view
empty	pass		

Content Vocabulary

approximate*	corner	middle	site
balance*	departure	partial*	solution*
commission*	difference*	period*	survey
constant*	entire	project*	system*
contest	investment	results*	value

Grades 10 and 11

Test Directions Vocabulary

effect*	example	strategy*
estimate*	situation*	substitute*

*English and Spanish cognates

Test Question Verbs

broke	expect	model*	pick
contradict*	hire	observe*	price
depend*	invalidate	occur*	reduce*
elapse	label	paint	win
enlarge	misplace		

Content Vocabulary

account	dependent*	kneel	portion*
arrangement	enlargement	label	projection*
blueprint	enrollment	loan	raise
borrow	foundation	multiple*	random
combination*	functional*	opposite*	reaction*
completely*	geoboard	original*	reduction*
completion	independent*	owner	sibling
consecutive*	inequality	peg	vacant*
container			

*English and Spanish cognates

Appendix B: Science Academic Word Lists for English Language Learners

Middle School

Test Directions Vocabulary

according to*	diagram*	follow	pattern*
based on*	document*	following	probably*
behavior	example	include*	record*
bubble	except*	information*	represent*
conclusion*	expect	knowledge	responsible*
describe*	fill in	most likely	table
determine*	find	object*	

Test Question Verbs

add	decrease*	follow	plant*
attack*	describe*	form*	produce*
build	design*	gain	product*
burn	destroy*	glow	project*
catch	determine*	guarantee*	question
cause*	difference*	handle	raise
change *	divide*	include*	reduce*
claim	evaporate*	information*	respond*
compare*	express*	measure	result*
conduct*	extinguish*	mix	run
continue*	find	occur*	separate*

*English and Spanish cognates

Test Question Verbs (continued)

control*	float	place	use*
create*			

Content Vocabulary

activity*	excess*	pressure	study*
balance*	factor*	range	sum*
chemical	force	rare	surface
control*	friction*	reaction*	system*
cycle*	front	relationship	table
data*	gram*	result*	thrust
decrease*	gravity	safety	vapor
direction*	habitat*	sample	volume*
electrical*	mass	section*	waste
energy*	model*	solution*	work
environment	order*	speed	

*English and Spanish cognates

Grade 9

Test Directions Vocabulary

characteristics*	experiment*	involve	reasonable*
characterize*	illustrate*	item	situation*
consider*	illustration*	procedure*	typical*
demonstrate*	inference*	process*	various*
effective*	investigation*		

Test Question Verbs

act*	cross	increase*	pump
advantage	discharge	induce*	react
affect*	display	inherit	reject
allow	dissolve*	introduce	release
apply	double*	isolate	remove
avoid	draw	lead	require
belong	drift	lower	search
benefit	eliminate*	melt	sour
break down	ensure	monitor	spray
calculate*	examine*	mutate	spread
collect*	exhibit*	observe*	stretch
combine*	expect	obtain*	supply
concentrate*	expose*	operate*	survive
confer	flow	overexpose	suspend
construct	function*	pose	torn
contain*	go off	pour	transfer*
convert*	go out	power	transport*

*English and Spanish cognates

Test Question Verbs (continued)

cover	identify*	prove	ventilate*
crack	ignite	provide	wear

Content Vocabulary

acceleration*	dominant*	mixture	representative*
access*	element*	momentum*	resistance*
action*	emission*	motion	secondary*
agent*	equation*	mutation*	sediment*
alloy	experiment*	nature	segment*
angle*	exposure	niche*	setup
appendage	fatal*	offspring	severe*
appropriate	fluid*	organism*	single
atmosphere*	formula*	outer	site
atomic*	frequency*	output	solvent*
biological*	genetic*	peak	species
bonding	harm, harmful	percentage*	strand
calorie*	hazard	physical*	substance*
cell*	hypothesis*	polar*	tertiary
circuit*	identical*	pollution*	threat
complement*	in relation to*	potential*	trait
composition*	increase*	power	ultraviolet*
compound	initial*	precaution*	unknown
compression*	input	presence*	upper
concentration*	interaction*	primary*	variable*
conservation*	irritation*	process*	velocity*
consumer*	joint	producer*	virus*
convection*	kinetic*	proper	visible*
core	lack	radiation*	voltage*

*English and Spanish cognates

Content Vocabulary (continued)

current*	layer	reactant	wave
defect*	lower	receptacle	web
density*	marker*	receptor*	weightless
destruction*	mechanical*	recessive*	

Grades 10 and 11

Test Directions Vocabulary

reasonably*			

Test Question Verbs

accomplish	erupt	precipitate*	transcribe*
assume*	expand*	prepare*	transform*
consist*	extract*	secure	transplant*
consistent*	generate*	solidify*	uncombined
deposit*	left over	suppress	vary*
displace	pluck	tear	violate*

Content Vocabulary

abnormal*	medium*	plentiful	suspension*
bombard*	molten	poison	teardrop
diversity*	nutrient*	productivity*	trace
infection*	onset	replication	vertical*
lunar*	particle*	rigid*	vital*

*English and Spanish cognates

Appendix C: Social Studies Academic Word Lists for English Language Learners

Middle School

Test Directions Vocabulary

according to*	diagram*	illustrate*	point of view
answer	difference*	image*	purpose
based on*	discuss	importance*	question
cartoon	document*	in part*	quotation
characterize*	excerpt*	incorrect*	result*
choose	express*	indicate*	significance*
complete*	fill in	knowledge	summarize*
conclude*	following	likely	table
conclusion*	graph*	match	timeline
correct*			

*English and Spanish cognates

Test Question Verbs

abandon*	develop	increase*	protect*
abolish*	discover*	influence*	provide*
acquire*	disregard	invent*	publish*
admit*	effect*	justify*	reduce*
aim	enable	lack	refer*
allow	encourage	lead	reform*
anger	enforce	limit*	regard
appoint	ensure	lower	rely
attack*	establish*	maintain*	remain
attempt	exceed*	mark*	remove
balance*	experience*	obtain*	represent*
benefit*	extend*	oppose	require*
clarify*	factor*	organize*	result*
consider*	favor*	outlaw	rise
continue*	force	pace	serve*
convert*	form*	pass*	slow
convince*	fortified*	perform	struggle
create*	found	permit*	support
deal	gain	prevent*	take part
declaring*	give up	produce*	tend
decline	grant	prohibit*	transport*
decrease*	guarantee	promote*	vote*
demand*	import*	prompt	

*English and Spanish cognates

Content Vocabulary

ability*	economy*	locomotive*	regulation*
abolition*	efficient*	man-made	removal
abolitionist*	election*	manufacture	representation*
act*	equal*	method*	right
activity*	establishment*	military*	role*
agricultural*	executive*	mouth (of river)	rule
amendment	expansion*	movement*	segregation*
annexation*	export*	national*	self-governing
appearance*	factory	nationalism*	settlement
army*	electoral*	natural resource	significant*
article*	failure	neutral*	skilled
authority*	federal*	office*	slave
believer	fertile*	opponent*	slavery
bill	foreign	party	solidly
branch	front	passage*	source
candidate*	fugitive*	patriot*	sovereignty
citizen	game	patriotism*	steamboat
citizenship	goods	plantation*	suffrage
civil*	government*	policy*	system*
colonial*	growth	politic*	tariff*
colony*	heading	political*	tax
compact*	immigrant*	population*	temperance*
competition*	immigration*	port	territory*
confederation*	independence*	present-day	textiles*
constitution*	industrial*	president*	timber
continental*	industry	presidential*	trade
convention*	injustice*	price	trail

*English and Spanish cognates

Content Vocabulary (continued)

cottage industry	interchangeable	primary*	treatment*
cotton gin	invasion*	production*	unalienable*
country	invention*	profit	unconstitutional*
court	issue	protective*	unequal*
declaration*	labor*	public*	union*
dependence*	leader*	publicly*	upheld
development	legislative	railroad	widespread
discovery*	levying	rapid*	
economic*	liberty*	region*	

Grade 9

Test Directions Vocabulary

associate*	dominate*	frame of reference	reflect*
characteristics*	draw conclusion	headline	

Test Question Verbs

access*	implement*	migrate*	reveal*
concentrate*	improve	pardon*	safeguard
declare*	isolate	proclaim*	seize
demonstrate*	locate*	reject	settle
eliminate*			

*English and Spanish cognates

Content Vocabulary

abundance*	compromise*	industrialize*	republicanism*
accountability	consumer*	legislator*	resource
administration*	contribution*	literacy	restriction*
agriculture*	crisis*	market	setback
assembly	cult*	migration*	settler
assumption*	delegate*	milestone	sovereign*
barrier*	democracy*	nationalize*	subsistence*
bias	dictatorship	offensive*	substantial*
border	diplomat*	official*	treaty
boundary	diplomatic*	output	tribunal*
censorship	dominant*	overproduction	unskilled
century	drought	period*	urban*
civilian*	ethnic*	poll	victory*
civilization*	excessive*	press	wage
coalition*	geographic*	regal	waterway
commerce*	imperialism*	republic*	

Grades 10 and 11

Test Directions Vocabulary

generally*	response*	theme

*English and Spanish cognates

Test Question Verbs

adhere*	diminish*	minimize*	resist*
assume*	dwindle	occur*	retain*
bolster	endanger	orient*	secure*
commit	exclude*	overextend	suspect
conserve*	expel*	pressure	threat
cooperate*	explore*	ratify	uphold
dealt	falter	rebuild	urge*
deport*	focus*	repeal*	
desegregate*	lay claim		

Content Vocabulary

account	depression*	funding	scale
affair	descendant*	impact*	scandal*
alliance*	diversity*	legitimate*	shareholders
assassination*	draft	neutrality*	stock
campaign*	embargo*	overcrowded	stock market
communism*	enterprise	pollution*	strike
communist*	environment	poverty	subjugation
conservation*	expectancy	ratification*	submarine*
corollary*	expedition*	regional*	threat
corps	federalism*	reliance	tolerance*
crucial*	forum*	ruling	welfare
demonstration*			

*English and Spanish cognates

References and Resources

Allen, J. (1999). *Words, words, words*. York, ME: Stenhouse Publishers.

Appleby, J., Brinkley, A., Broussard, A. S., McPherson, J. M., & Ritchie, D. A. (2003). *The American republic since 1877*. New York: Glencoe McGraw-Hill.

Beck, I. L. (2002). *Bringing words to life*. New York: The Guilford Press.

Berenstain, S., & Berenstain, J. (1997). *Inside, outside, upside down*. New York: Random House.

Bielenberg, B., & Fillmore, L. W. (2004, December/2005, January). The English they need. *Educational Leadership, 62*(4), 45–49.

Blachowicz, C., & Fisher, P. J. (2002). *Teaching vocabulary in all classrooms*. Upper Saddle River, NJ: Pearson Education.

Boehm, R. G. (2003). *World geography* (Teacher wraparound ed.). New York: Glencoe McGraw-Hill.

Boyd, C. D. (2005). *Building a nation: Social studies* (Teacher ed.). Upper Saddle River, NJ: Pearson Education.

Chamot, U., & O'Malley, J. M. (1994). *The CALLA handbook*. New York: Addison-Wesley.

Coxhead, A. (2000). A new academic word list. *TESOL Quarterly, 34*(2), 213–238.

Coxhead, A., & Nation, P. (2001). The specialised vocabulary of English for academic purposes. In J. Flowerdew and M. Peacock, *Research perspectives on English for academic purposes* (pp. 252–267). Cambridge, England: Cambridge University Press.

Cummins, J. (1983). Language proficiency and academic achievement. In J. W. Oller, Jr. (Ed.), *Issues in language testing research* (pp. 108–129). Rowley, MA: Newbury House.

Davidson, J. W., & Underwood, K. (1992). *American journey: The quest for liberty to 1877* (Texas ed.). Needham, MA: Prentice Hall.

Echevarria, J., Short, D. J., & Vogt, M. (2004). *Making content comprehensible for English language learners*. Upper Saddle River, NJ: Pearson Education.

Ellis, E. G., & Esler, A. (2003). *World history: Connections to today*. New York: Glencoe McGraw-Hill.

Jacob, L. (1866). The Freemen's Record. In r4 Educated Solutions, *TAKS social studies preparation grade 10*. Houston, TX: Author.

Marzano, R. J. (2004). *Building background knowledge for academic achievement*. Alexandria, VA: Association for Supervision and Curriculum Development.

Marzano, R. J. (2005). *Building academic vocabulary*. Alexandria, VA: Association for Supervision and Curriculum Development.

Numeroff, L. J. (1997). *If you give a mouse a cookie*. New York: HarperCollins Children's Books.

r4 Educated Solutions. (2005). *Accelerated curriculum for social studies, grade 11*. Houston, TX: Author.

r4 Educated Solutions. (2006). *Reading to learn in social studies, grades 6-8*. Houston, TX: Author.

Whitehurst, G. J. (2002). *Evidence-based education (EBE)*. Presentation at the Student Achievement and School Accountability Conference, Orlando, FL. Accessed at ed.gov/nclb/methods/whatworks/eb/edlite-slide003.html on July 4, 2006.

Index

Solution Tree | Press

a division of

Solution Tree

Solution Tree's mission is to advance the work of our authors. By working with the best researchers and educators worldwide, we strive to be the premier provider of innovative publishing, in-demand events, and inspired professional development designed to transform education to ensure that all students learn.

The core purpose of Region 4 is revolutionizing education to inspire and advance future generations™. Instructional materials such as this publication are written and reviewed by content-area specialists who have an array of experience in providing quality, effective classroom instruction that provides the most impact on student achievement.

Making Math Accessible for English Language Learners Series
By r4 Educated Solutions
Build the academic language English language learners need to gain proficiency in mathematics. These practical classroom tips and suggestions provide a solid plan for bringing disadvantaged learners up to speed with essential vocabulary while keeping the entire class engaged with the lessons.

Grades K–2	Grades 3–5	Grades 6–8	Grades 9–12
BKF284	BKF285	BKF286	BKF287

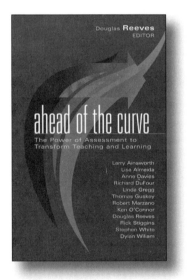

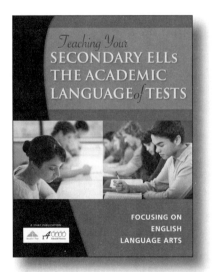

Ahead of the Curve: The Power of Assessment to Transform Teaching and Learning
Edited by Douglas Reeves
Get the anthology that offers the ideas and recommendations of many of the world's leaders in assessment. Many perspectives of effective assessment design and implementation culminate in a call for redirecting assessment to improve student achievement and inform instruction.
BKF232

Teaching Your Secondary English Language Learners the Academic Language of Tests: Focusing on English Language Arts
By r4 Educated Solutions
Teach your English language learners unfamiliar language features before they are encountered in core content areas and standardized test questions. Evidence-based, teacher-friendly lesson plans also support content-area teachers in providing instruction for content-specific language skills.
BKF292